THE ENCHANTING CONTRADICTION

MEMORIES OF THE MIDDLE EAST

Patricia Heurtaux

iUniverse, Inc.
Bloomington

The Enchanting Contradiction
Memories of the Middle East

iUniverse books may be ordered through booksellers or by contacting:

iUniverse
1663 Liberty Drive
Bloomington, IN 47403
www.iuniverse.com
1-800-Authors (1-800-288-4677)

ISBN: 978-1-4620-2255-7 (sc)
ISBN: 978-1-4620-2256-4 (hc)
ISBN: 978-1-4620-2257-1 (e)

Printed in the United States of America

iUniverse rev. date: 06/01/2011

For Camille, to remember

For Mouhiddine, who lit up my sky

For my friends, that I love

Special thanks to Justin for helping me with the translation.

Contents

PREFACE

A lot is happening in the Middle-East right now. Definitely, changes are coming in, but before the life were quite peaceful and joyful. Terrorists, extremists, Jihad...are some of the words that are now commonly associated with the Middle-East and Islam; but as the saying goes, there are another side to every story. After spending several years in Dubai, the need to write about what were our lives in this part of the world appears obvious.

"The Enchanting Contradiction" is a compilation of memories, perceptions and criticisms too, but we properly criticize only those we love. Not being an expert on the world situation and geo-political matters, especially the Arab world, but being a woman who has a brain and a heart, I claim the right to express my perceptions and analyses; after all, they belong to me.

A sincere apology to anyone who feels discriminated or hurt by any means; be sure it was not my intention; only for the freedom of speech.

As a French conservative *bourgeoise,* the life I spent in the United Arab Emirates opened my eyes and my mind. Setting up a lot of foreign companies in this country, the lesson of adaptability, flexibility, patience and understanding was crucial. It has shifted my way to respect other people from another background and nobody detains the unmistakable truth.

After making a very good career in the business and having a lot of hobbies, I was diagnosed with multiple sclerosis. It changed drastically the life, from being extremely busy I became disabled without my legs, arms and hands working anymore. Rather to feel sorry, I chose to write stories.

Here is the story of a unique woman who, with her seven years old daughter in tow, took a chance and lived in the Middle-East for more than a decade. Let yourself be charmed by her bittersweet and humorous recollection of the best years of her life as she came to know *The Enchanting Contradiction* that is the Middle-east.

I DESPISE NARROW MINDS: THERE YOU FIND
NOTHING GOOD AND ALMOST NOTHING BAD.

NIETZSCH

CHAPTER 1

Departing for the United Arab Emirates

D UE TO A PAINFUL divorce and a "no happy end love story", it was very hard to stay in France. Somewhere it was over and I wanted to flee, therefore I decided to take one of the biggest challenges in my life: Leave my country and try another life with my new boyfriend in Dubai. So, one day of July 1992, my daughter and I, were ready for the farewell.

It was a gloomy and sticky day at the airport. I felt a pain in the pit of my stomach, but I smiled; I smiled for my daughter, I smiled for my mother, letting them know that I took the right decision. I tried to soothe my mother's heart; she was watching us leaving everything behind to go to a faraway and unknown country, full of weird stories. I had to convince my daughter that she was about to discover an exciting new place, full of promises, and she'd come back to France to spend her vacations with her father.

But how could I find the right words when I was afraid of this unknown? When the Middle-East had such bad reputation, how could I explain to my mother that it was, in fact, a wonderful destination, especially Dubai and it would be a perfect new beginning? Was I irresponsible? Was it too much challenge for my daughter to leave the country where she was born, her brothers and sisters, her friends and all the familiar surroundings? She was so young.

I asked her "Do you remember last summer when we went to Dubai?

"Yes"

"It was so enjoyable wasn't it and you had so much fun"

"Yes"

"We are going to see the same people you were playing with, and we'll go back to the same beach club."

"Yes, but I am going to a new school and to lose all my friends."

"Don't worry sweetheart, I think very quickly you'll have new friends, and your new teacher is very nice. You'll see the school is lovely."

Two big blue eyes looked at me and what I saw inside moved my heart and my soul. There was distress, resignation, but also an unconditional love and trust.

"Don't worry honey, you won't be alone. I've decided to work in the French school where you're going. We'll go together and you'll know that I'll be next to you"

Finally a smile brightened her face and her tiny hand grabbed mine. I felt nauseous and scared. *Leaving everything behind* was harder than I thought.

At this time, in 1992, very few people knew about Dubai or the United Arab Emirates (U.A.E). It seemed like two worlds apart, even though it was only a six hours flight from Paris. A little country tucked away between Oman and Saudi Arabia. Everything I heard did not matter once we landed. I was completely under the spell. So much, so that this country will forever be etched in my memory and my heart.

Nothing was easy, but everything was interesting, forcing me to reassess my beliefs and perceptions. Living there, we had to quickly abandon all our Western notions and pre-convinced ideas, to learn from a new place with different customs, values and traditions.

Over there, time is relative, flexible. Everything is done at a slower pace, more gently. Smiles are everywhere and they penetrate all your defenses. The concept of taking your time, meeting people, enjoying life and letting go, is a real philosophy.

It seems that bright sunny skies have the power to lessen metaphysical pains and suffering. Here, we're more concerned about whether the AC works than finding answers to our existential questions.

This kind of "take-it-easy" ambiance has helped Camille and me a lot in dealing with my mother's death, her father's death, my disease (multiple sclerosis) and other setbacks and painful situations. It opened the door to another side of life: more joyful, more hopeful.

As I said, nothing was really easy, not even the new beginning. The man I liked, who was partly responsible for my move to Dubai, wanted to marry me but he would have preferred for Camille to live with his father. So here I am, torn between the love for this man and the unconditional love I have for my daughter. After a whole night of sobbing, looking more like a frog than a human being, I decided to get rid of this relationship. My daughter was more important and living apart from her was out of question.

So we drifted apart; he began a new relationship with a Lebanese woman and I fell into the arms of the philosophy teacher working at the French School. I must say it was epic! He wasn't so much a lover as an amateur psychiatrist who must have spent his free time reading Russian KGB manuals. It was endless interrogations, pointless attempts to solve existential problems and his childish sulking if I did not give him the right answer.

In fact, he was looking for the solution to his own issues. I really suspected he was sexually and psychologically abused by his mother, which affected his view on women and made it impossible for him to engage in healthy and romantic relationships. In the end, after six months of a relationship that felt more like seeing a shrink than having a boyfriend, he left me for the maid!!! Very common, I know, but it hurts so bad your ego, your feelings, your self confidence and your dreams.

So there, I was devastated and depressed for losing my hope for a new happiness, wishing I was dead, until one unforgettable night. Some friends had taken me camping in the desert, in the hope of cheering me up, when staring at this incredible sky, we saw a shooting star.

"Make a wish" one of them said.

"Last time I made a wish, it ended badly, so I am going to pass" I replied.

"Of course it ended badly. At the same time your boyfriend was thinking: I'd really like to nail the maid".

Put this way, I realized how ridiculous the whole situation was and I started to laugh hysterically. And that was it. I was back on track, not fully healed but getting there.

Unfortunately, when I got home life had another surprise for me. My ex-husband called, in tears; he had just been diagnosed with colon cancer. It was a complete electric shock. A new battle was beginning and I needed all my energy to fight it. No more whining and complaining; how could I be depressed when the man I loved the most, the father of my child, was fighting with death, how to talk to my daughter and prepare her to the worst. He battled like a brave and positive soldier for six years before leaving for another journey.

Life, most of the time, send some signs to put you back in your shoes and to help you to see what is essential. Perhaps, because, I didn't understand that fully, it came back to me when my mother was also diagnosed with cancer. As she didn't keep a positive mind, she left one year after. We should listen more carefully our inner voice, rather to ignore it and to pretend.

CHAPTER 2

When prejudice influences our perception

I F I MADE A list of the most preconceived notions about the Arab world, it would look something like this:

-The Middle East: A huge desert with only sand, rocks, wandering camels, sandstorms, mirages, thirst and heat.

-Arabs: Uncivilized Bedouins that either live in a cave or under a tent with camels and goats for company. Of course, most of people don't differentiate between Arabs, Persians and North Africans who speak different dialects and have different cultures; but after all, it's only a detail.

-Islam: An extremist religion that ignores basic human rights, idolizes Allah and breeds terrorists blinded by violence and thirst for revenge. (Don't fool yourself thinking that what is going on in Europe is the spread of fundamentalist muslims. Muslims, black people, and any foreign minorities were never really integrated among the conservative population. What is happening now, is generated by the youth who is the second generation born in Europe; they are just fed up with the discrimination and living in ghettos. So far, over there, have you seen any colored or muslim chief of government?)

At the time, in 1992, this basically summed up the ideas and opinions of people who did not know the Middle East (still now). They were all ignorant, but at least they subscribed to the same stereotypes. I always find it pathetic how some people can pretend to be experts just because, they watch the news and read the papers; they forget to think or question themselves and use their brain wisely. It's quite terrifying to hear such closed-minded opinions from people who claim to be highly educated.

The first thing I learned when I tried my story was; you can't teach people who lack the curiosity and desire to learn. It is as difficult as convincing an agoraphobic that's safe to stand in the middle of a crowd. As I was not Freud or Lacan, I let it go…

When I was coming to Europe, because I guess of my attitude, a lot of people were often talking to me. Try to picture anyone who was asking me where I lived:

"Dubai"

"Where is that?"

"In the Middle East"

(Wide eyes, mouth opened, blank expression)

"Between Saudi Arabia and Iran"

(Now, the blank expression turns into utter terror)

"So, you're covered up…"

"No, I am dressed normally"

"Can you go out?"

"No, I'm looked up in a dungeon guarded by a fiery dragon" was what I wanted to answer, but to keep things simple, I just respond:

"Yes, I go out, I work, I drive and I raise my daughter"

"All by yourself! It must be so hard for a single woman to live there"

"Well, I must be a real masochist because I have been living there for many years"

Of course, it was not so easy to make it in a male dominated society but it teaches to be more creative, resourceful and to keep up my ego on standby.

Instead of my explosive temperament I had to adopt a softer, calmer attitude and to learn a new necessary virtue: patience. You see, life in the Middle East is punctuated by the almighty *Inch Allah* (God willing), *Bukkra* (tomorrow) which can either be tomorrow, in one week or never. Although I adapted quickly, I must admit that on several occasions I just totally lost it!

For instance, I remember our air conditioning shutting off (because of a power cut) in the middle of July, when temperatures are about 120oF. I had to wait more than 24 hours before they even sent someone out to take a look at it. I thought I would go insane, being even unable to take a cold shower (you can't get cold water in the summer because the water tanks are mounted on the roof). I ended up going berserk and moving over to a friend's house. Thank God, my daughter was in France.

I had also a couple of issues with the local administration (but who doesn't have some?) It is interesting that through my travels I have never had a pleasant administrative experience (try the DMV in the U.S.A or the Social Security offices in France and you'll know what I am talking about). It is belief that people who work in the public services are a special underground breed, especially trained to excel at ruining people's lives. They seem to be born frustrated, hating everyone and only getting pleasure from other people's humiliation and anger. Their sex life must be boring or nil.

It gets even more complicated in the Middle East where men and women can't mix. You have a special public department for women, run only by females who wear traditional clothes (*abaya* and *shila*). They tend to dislike Western women because, no matter how many layers of clothes we're wearing, we're still showing more skin than they do. This doesn't make communication any easier!

Over there, the concept of time is different and doesn't have the same value as in the West. Nothing is worse than showing impatience and aggressiveness: it goes against Eastern customs and creates an atmosphere of mistrust…

We, Westerners tend to think that our culture prevails over that of other countries. We see ourselves highly educated and civilized, and as such we know everything and have all the answers (even if they are false). We want the world as we picture it, even if this picture doesn't suit other countries and our trust is biased.

Our culture is neither better nor worse; it is simply different from the one in the Middle East or the Far East. Moreover, the West is much diversified and each Western country is quite specific unto itself, with its traditions, history and influences.

I have lived in France, England, Germany, Greece and now I've settled permanently in the USA, so I am able to experience the cultural dissimilarities within the West. It would be nice if one day, we could realize that our customs and reference points are our own perceptions, and that these perceptions reflect only our culture. In the Middle East those perceptions and opinions are not the same. Knowing the Arab world for more than 18 years helps me to have a more accurate view on what is the best and the worst, and on all kinds of contradictions.

These experiences have also taught me that ignorance breeds fear. The unknown always frightens us and appears menacing because we have to guess what to expect, not knowing what to anticipate. With today's technology and globalization, it should be easier for us to do research, read or hear about different opinions and communicate with people from other cultures, instead of being blinded by our fear and preconceived notions.

However, getting truthful, impartial information is often difficult, especially with respect to the Middle East. The media and politicians would have us believe anything that best serves their interests; a truly "free press" is a utopia.

The media are subject to governmental pressures, and many journalists who first set out to report "the Truth" are either shut down or pushed into more conventional reporting. So we are mostly fed with gossip and commercialized photos of celebrities on the beach, taking out the garbage, cheating on their spouses and so on. News is boring and does not sell as well as V.I.P's private lives. Even they have issues, it's so reassuring. There's a popular saying: "divide and conquer"; it's always easier to manage a herd of sheep (a herd of calves, said General de Gaulle) by removing their capacity of critical thought.

In my personal utopia, I would like to receive clear, impartial and truthful information and news. I would also like politicians and the media to give more credit to the people. We can think, we can handle it. If we could analyze clearly and freely, would it lead to chaos? I don't think so.

CHAPTER 3

Arriving in Dubai

W E LANDED LATE AT night. There's a three hours time difference with France in the winter and two hours in the summer. It was so hot and humid that it was like putting our heads into an oven. Finally we got in the shuttle and everything seemed better thanks to the AC.

When we went through immigration, the officer made a point to welcome us in French. The power of a smile is so obvious. We were both tired but happy to be there. The knot in my stomach was still upsetting me but tomorrow would be another day, and things would be just fine. I just wanted to sleep and pulled myself together. On the drive home, I stared silently out of the window, unable to talk. There were so many things tumbling over one another in my mind. That fear; I was so afraid I made the wrong choice, having disrupted my daughter's life for the worse. Did I act with her best interests in mind or was I just being selfish? (Almost two decades later, I can say it was the best decision ever. I have so amazing memories).

The next day, although it was very hot (120oF) and humid (96%), we decided to get acquainted with our new city.

Dubai is on the Arabian Gulf and surrounded by desert. We were very surprised to see trees and flowers everywhere. In fact, the U.A.E imports a lot of trees (eucalyptus, acacia, bougainvillea, frangipani and hibiscus) and grass. They dedicate a lot of money and effort to creating an efficient irrigation system. They even have golf clubs that use about 250,000 gallons of water each day. The factories which process the salty water into still water work non-stop. In July, The palm trees are stuffed with dates, the bougainvilleas are blooming with red, yellow, purple and white flowers and the scent of frangipanis fills the air.

In 1993, the country was just starting to emerge. The French school was located in Sharjah, a neighboring emirate, the French community was fairly small, and only 30% of the students were of French origin.

The remainder was Lebanese, Syrian, Belgian, Canadian and so on. With every skin color and multiple languages, the French school looked like the Tower of Babel, but the atmosphere was relaxed and fun. We even had a French Consul who was originally from India and whose wife wore a sari to all the Consulate receptions!

Because of this diversity the French school had mandatory English and Arabic classes from Middle school to 12th grade. Even if the official language is Arabic, most of people speak English (the U.A.E was a British colony). These classes got incredible results, leading most children to be bilingual or trilingual (plus, in the French system, in the 8th grade, students have to take one or two foreign languages). It was a great program to stimulate children's brains and open up their minds to another dimension. Even though my school days were far behind me, I had to become a student again to refresh my English and to learn Arabic. So, there I was, partly Jewish on my father's side, partly Catholic on my mother's side, who used to live a very comfortable life among high society, artists, intellectuals and politicians, leaving it all behind to move to an unknown country with my suitcases, my daughter and my cat "Lola". That was when I remembered a quote: "adaptability is the true intelligence of human kind". Let's adapt then.

CHAPTER 4

The differences

WHEN YOU GET TO the UAE, you have to adopt many new customs, ranging from the dress code, how to introduce yourself, eat, have fun and socialize.

Starting with the clothing

The Emirati men wear the traditional white robe (*deshdash*) and cover their head with a scarf (*keffieh*) that is either solid white or checkered, depending on their origin, which is held in place by a black band (*guttra*). They look very proud with those garments.

The Emirati women, in most cases, wear a thin black coat (*abaya*) and hide their hair with a black veil (*shila*). Depending on their origin and traditions, some of them are completely covered or wear a leather mask to hide their nose and mouth. Once only, I had to wear the abaya and shila when I was invited to the Iranian Club. Otherwise, expatriates (Muslim or not) are not obliged to wear traditional clothing. You can do whatever you want as long as you maintain a certain level of decency. Nevertheless, we've seen women walking around with tiny shorts and low cut tank tops. It was not a major problem except the fact I heard some nasty comments because they obviously lacked any kind of respect or consideration for a culture that was welcoming them with open arms. In Europe, you easily recognize low class American tourists;

they always wear flashy shorts and tee-shirts with either sneakers or flip-flops.

In the UAE, women can drive, work, go shopping, go out and enjoy many other activities freely. The only restrictions are in the salons, spas, and fitness clubs where men and women are separated. At least we are not bothered by the stares and comments of horny men! That being said I practiced Martial Arts for years in a co-ed club and the equestrian center where my daughter used to ride was also co-ed. The best example was in the school, where boys and girls from all skin colors and religions were mixed.

Indeed, the UAE are quite liberal and are more progressive than other Arab countries (except Lebanon). There is no religious police ready to arrest you if you show your knees, just a disapproving look and some comments that you've gone too far. In this matter, I always have supported the UAE because I find utterly disrespectful and intolerant to ignore the basic principles of another country which welcomes you. For instance, it's customary for Middle Easterners to burp after a good meal. It's a way to let you know that the meal was good and they are satiated. What would be your reaction if they were doing that in your Western world?, (unless, of course you don't have manners).

About driving,

Even though they drive on the right side of the road, like I was used to, driving in the UAE is a real challenge and it took me six months of being terrified before I got accustomed to it. Every time I made it from A to B in one piece, I thanked God for this miracle! Today, still I am worried when my daughter has to drive.

To put all this in perspective, here are some facts: 60% of the population comes from India, Pakistan, Sri Lanka and the Philippines, 20% migrates from other parts of Middle East, Eastern Europe and Western countries; only 20% are native Emiratis.

Now, take into account that Indians are used to driving on the left side (thanks to the Brits for that), therefore, they will consistently drive at slow speed in the left lane (which is supposed to be the fastest one) and then suddenly cut across all of the lanes to their exit, which is located on the right side! (Floridians do the same, although they were not under British influence!?!?). That creates a very good quick reaction drill and a sure way to test your brakes. To that, add the fact that not so long ago, Emiratis were riding camels; so they jumped from their saddle to their car seat with no driving school test to get their driving license! Most of them drive powerful cars or big SUV's, and to finish it off, mix into it the various driving styles of all the other expatriates and there you have it. Ah! I almost forgot: over there blinkers and mirrors are usually seen as optional accessories to make their cars prettier, and they are often afraid to hurt their fingers by using them (it reminds me again Florida). Most of people don't even use them or leave those blinkers on indefinitely, just because they like it when their car blinks, or maybe the sound enchants them. So, basically the driving style comes down to holding the steering wheel, stepping on the gas, and braking when you can't do otherwise.

The favorite game is to drive on the highway, as if you were in a NASCAR race: going full speed, coming so close to the car in front of you that you're almost on the top of it, and driving on the median or emergency breakdown lane to go faster. In the Western world, you have bungee jumping or sky diving; here we drive to get the same powerful sensations.

Now, let's talk about eating.

What a variety! In 1993, there were no large grocery stores, only a few small Arab or Indian supermarkets, so we had a limited choice of vegetables and fruits. Goodbye baguette and stinky cheese, instead we found pita bread, yogurt (*labneh*) fresh cheese, eggs, milk made from powder, anemic chicken, lamb, delicious fish and rice (a lot).

My daughter complained about the lack of dairy products, desserts and chocolate. She was fond of delicacies but she adapted to the new diet. For school I prepared some snacks with pita, labneh and cucumber. We mainly ate Indian or Arabic food and discovered new flavors and tastes. Of course some tummy upsets occurred, but many unknown spices and herbs enticed our palate in a good way.

The restaurants we went to, offered a large variety of excellent food for very reasonable prices with service and kindness that I never found anywhere else. They all pride themselves on satisfying all of their customers.

Indeed, in the Middle East, hospitality is an important tradition and even the poor will offer food and drink to welcome you into their home. You will never leave hungry but the trick is to avoid getting indigestion.

A close friend of mine, a dermatologist, who used to visit us every year, had to face a situation which pleased me quite a bit. One of my Arab acquaintances had asked me about effective remedies for his daughter's acne. So, I arranged a consultation with my friend and we went together to his home. First surprise, the decoration of his villa was from another world. We could see cuddly toys everywhere. A bear's cuddly skin was on the floor in the lobby with under its mouth, a plastic hand!!! In the living room, right in the middle: a gigantic green octopus. I could not look at my friend, afraid to burst in laugh. It was a good start for a memorable night. After the consultation, to show us his gratitude, he invited us to his restaurant. I am quite sure that he ordered every single item on the menu as our table was constantly filled with food. My friend tasted everything. As the night went on, I could see her little waistcoat rising up and up her breast and her belly becoming a very visible bump. I could not eat as much as she, but I laughed a lot.

In the Middle East, when you want to honor your guests, you must prepare 11 different dishes. It's hard for staying slender but so good for the palate and warm for the heart.

What about entertainment, are you wondering?

Although we lived in Dubai, the other emirates and neighboring countries offered awesome landscapes with an unspoiled natural beauty (unfortunately, not for very long, as you will see below). This beauty so vivid was ample compensation for the lack of TV and movie theaters. Yes, you can trust me on this; it was the end of the 20th century!

In the UAE, the color of the sea has nuances from turquoise to deep blue. The beach is made on thin white sand on the west coast and dark grey on the east one. The mountains are layered with a subtle mix of brown, pink and green, and of course the desert plays with white sand near the beach until it becomes red inland. There are lascivious and sensual dunes forming sometimes, the shape of an elongated woman's body. On the crest of those dunes, we can contemplate the immenseness of the landscape with the wind as our only friend. Suddenly, here, you feel infallible and for a moment, we touch lightly upon eternity, with feet on the ground and head in the clouds.

In the desert, nothing is more breathtaking than the ambiance at sunrise and sunset. You have the feeling that you are part of the landscape and that nothing bad can happen or harm you: a moment of complete osmosis with the universe. A moment we'd like to keep, in order to fill ourselves with peace and serenity. Now and then, far away the muezzin's voice adds this divine spark that leads us to contemplation and to the awareness of the real sense of happiness.

Like kids, we were playing and driving in this sand, had flat tires, or broke some car parts in the middle of nowhere, but our mood was carefree and joyful, even though it took a long time to remedy our misfortunes. Often some Bedouins roaming in the dunes came to help us. We did not speak the same language but we shared solidarity and cheer. Once I got a flat tire on the top of a dune. We had arranged a

19

trip with two cars: one with the girls and the other one with the boys. The men rushed to help us, and took the jack and the spare tire. Keep in mind that changing a tire in the soft sand is a real challenge. However, we were with two engineers and normally this kind of guy has brain. So, they took out the front floor carpets, then squeezed the jack under the car, and puffed and panted for a few moments before removing the tire......Oooops! Once the tire was off, the car rocked and plunged deep into the sand. The girls chuckled, making comments about their IQ: yep! It was a no-no.

Happily, although you had the impression that desert meant loneliness and silence that was not true. Some Emiratis passing by offered their help. They got an inflatable cushion that they set underneath the car and plugged it to the exhaust pipe. It took 30 seconds to raise the car and put on the new tire. I found it outstanding and bought one right away. Here I am, in the city, and once again my tire burst. Therefore, proud of my cushion I just set it in place and started to blow it up, but suddenly, pffffffft, the cushion started deflating. I just forgot that on asphalt you could find nails and pieces of glass. This time, it was unsuccessful!

Most of the time, we stopped at dusk for camping. Each one had their tasks: taking out the coolers, preparing the fire, putting up the tents. The night falls pretty fast and our days were finished quite early. We ate, told stories, played and sang some music but overall, we were watching the sky: what a fabulous show! I have never seen since such a vivid sky. Perhaps, it's the same enchanting pleasure in the middle of the ocean or in the mountains. I was lucky to initiate my daughter to those new perspectives. She was caught by this country, despite its simplicity (this is hard and sentimentally dry) but its great charm.

CHAPTER 5

A little bit of history

ONCE UPON A TIME in the fifties, a village nestled in the sand called Dubai was inhabited by some Bedouins, pearl hunters, boat handymen and fishermen. At that time there was no luxury, but a lot of positivity and will to work hard. Those strong skills led them to build a solid and vibrant society. In no time, traders, retailers, teachers rushed in. Thank to this fast growth, you still can discover a delicate patina of nostalgia in the spirit of the elderly.

In 1993, Dubai had a population of 500,000. The only tall building (32 floors) was the Trade Center. There were only two lane roads and between each emirate, you could see a sandy desert no-man's land. No big hypermarkets, no movie theaters (to be precise, there was just one but it showed only Arabic or Indian movies), few hotels, some restaurants, one night club, two or three shopping malls and also some surprising *souks* (for fruits and vegetables, fish, gold, fabrics, spices, electronic appliances...)

The UAE has a long history as we follow the trail of human development for the past 5 000 years, but it was only in 1972 that the country federated into seven emirates (states): Abu Dhabi, Dubai, Sharjah, Ajman, Umm al Quwain, Ras el Rhaimah, Fujairah, and a government was born. Great Britain gave up this Gulf's territory in 1968; consequently the country's economy and government were quite young.

In the beginning the Bedouins were living frugally from trading pearls. When this market collapsed in 1930, they started oil exploitation and aluminum production. The first oil exportation took place in 1969. Since, the oil stock decreased, although Abu Dhabi still produces it, Dubai was obliged to find other alternatives for economic development (oil is only 5% of the GNP).

The strength in Dubai is the ruler's family (Al Maktoum) and especially Sheikh Mohammed (vice-president). He has a vision and welcomes ambitious challenges for Dubai. He dares to take some risky decisions and commits significant financial resources for Dubai to become a focus for trade and tourism. He plans also few laws to increase active participation from women; his wife, Princess Haya, will be one of the organizers for Horse jumping competitions during the next Olympic Games.

The UAE can be compared to Switzerland in Europe; this country is quite liberal, less than Lebanon but much more than Saudi Arabia, where as a woman I could not go.

The UAE adopt a progressive attitude, knowing that their oil reserves are not unlimited. Dubai, above all, is extremely ingenious in attracting people from around the world (trade, investment, real estate, tourism and so on).There are several free zones which facilitate international trade. The right to own a property began in 2000, which helped some expatriate take root. Still, there are some aspects which need to be improved, because if someone can buy a house, he is only the owner of the building, not of the land. Although, now it is a free hold law, you still have to obtain a residence visa, which is regulated by a government's decision (it's changing periodically!); The UAE don't abide by international laws; it's the Sh'aria laws which prevail.

In 2006, the inhabitants of Dubai increased to 1.3 million. Now, we find hypermarkets, movie theaters are mushrooming like crazy and the shopping malls compete which each other through luxurious excesses.

Regarding the real estate, we are facing an insane situation, the Burj Al Arab is a hotel built on an artificial island, Palm Islands were built in the sea in a palm tree shape, and, there is a new project to do the same with some islands configured in the shape of the world's atlas! (the economical crisis has stopped the construction). The traffic is becoming a nightmare and now we can ski on a huge snowy slope, located inside a shopping mall. Try to conceive that during summertime, the temperatures hit around 120oF, but inside this ski facility the temperature is kept at 30oF. It's better than going on the trip to the moon!

Now, the French school has moved to a bigger location in Dubai, due to the rapid development of the city and the increasing number of French expatriates. Unfortunately, this move has not been for the better. Many teachers report that the school atmosphere has radically changed: students are disrespectful, undisciplined and the teachers have joined the Union. Also American universities are bringing their knowledge and teachers in fantastic locations.

With this radicalism and speed of growth, the risk is at the same time economic, cultural and social:

-Economic, because the investments are chaotic and unstructured. I doubt that the long term return on investment was seriously taken into consideration; the cash spending looks like a gushing hemorrhage. I am not so sure that the surfeit of buildings, commercial structures and hotels can generate an immediate cash return, as Dubai is several billion dollars in debt. Prices are increasing in real estate, but also for food, and daily needs are cooling off reckless investors who wish to buy. The lifestyle is completely different; it's very hard now to save money and the people who earn the lowest salaries are facing miserable conditions.

The world economic crisis is shaking Dubai. Dubai is facing a kind of bankruptcy because its lack of cash and because of its unplanned and uncontrolled development. Right now, they are in a situation where they can't meet their payments and the debt is about seventy billion of dollars. Only Abu Dhabi can help (reluctantly) by lending or giving some money, in order to keep a stable situation for the UAE. The Maktoum family is not really keen to let go some of its properties in exchange, and Abu Dhabi is negotiating fiercely the bail out. It looks like Abu Dhabi will remain the most attractive spot in the future for huge agriculture progress, building museums and cultural centers, incredible resorts, a green city, sports centers and, as always, oil

-Human; as the Arab tradition is evolving toward a hybrid situation. It can be positive because we're meant to be mixed and to share our cultural landmarks. The only thing which saddens me is the risk of seeing the first heritage disappears. Hopefully, we'll remain aware and wise enough not to forget.

-Social, because I can see the relationship between people is changing. Before, it was smooth, even in the dryness of this country. We were all together; we had the talent for sharing. No one cared about your skin color, the religion you believed in or the social class you belonged to. That's not true any longer. Each one belongs to his own community. Before, it was over Arab *mechoui*, Iranian caviar, Indian *dal* and Filipino shrimps that we had our really joyful atmosphere.

CHAPTER 6

Everything went fast, but not without disappointment

A FTER SPENDING A YEAR teaching social and economic sciences, a Saudi company offered to hire me to set up some stores in the Middle East. At last, I found a good interesting job, well paid and pretty challenging. I had to establish a master franchisee structure in the Arab countries. In fact, I was also "adopted" into my family's boss. So quite quickly, I had to deal with my work but also with the friendly feeling which bound me to the family. Without any deliberate action on my part, but with my implicit approval, things became mixed up. I was invited very often for dinner, parties, and even week-ends.

We had a lot of fun, sometimes going to the desert, sometimes boating. We saw the first off-shore race from the sea. It was absolutely fascinating to see those water geysers and to hear those engines roaring like crazy. Hilarious detail: some Emiratis, wanting to enjoy the race from the closest spot, drove their Mercedes onto the beach and ended up in the water. The car engine did not like it at all; the car was almost floating.

I soon saw that aside from a few French friends, the French community distinguished itself by its absence and its lack of solidarity. I have to say that a pretty and smart single woman represents a big threat for these insecure "mamas". The best support I got came from few French friends (seldom) and some foreigners; some Emiratis were very kind and caring, they protected me without expecting anything in return.

Often, on Friday (day off) one of them was going to the fish market and brought me back some fresh fish, shrimps and so. I was lucky enough to meet other Middle Eastern people: Palestinian, Jordanian, Iranian, Iraqi, Egyptian, Syrian and Lebanese, who offered me spontaneous friendship. They adopted me and my daughter as well, just because in the Arab culture, you don't leave a single woman with a kid without help. It's against all the family principles defined in the Holy Koran.

Islam is not what ignorant people say. It is of course a difficult religion to understand and to comply with, but it's also a religion full of common sense, according how you interpret it. For example, the consumption of pork was forbidden because, at that time, this meat was not healthy. Regarding alcohol, it's quite obvious that you lose your self control when you're under its influence. The Koran is the Holy book which not only honors Allah and his prophet but, also gives some guidance and advice for walking through life's various pitfalls.

There are rules for hygiene, food and attitude. Most of the women are submissive and, some advice is given to them in order to dress with decency (no mention of *burqa* or total face covered), first to protect them from male harassment, secondly to give the same chance to the ugly and the beautiful ones. That said, quite often the choice comes from women! The relationship between men and women are not only based on sexual attraction but, more, on the influence of two families and the chemistry between two spirits and two temperaments. I'd like to recommend reading "The Prophet" by Khalil Gibran. It is a marvel of simplicity, yet of considerable depth. Of course, the Koran could be, like the Bible and the Torah, interpreted in so many different ways; most of the time it's through men understanding who very commonly fear the women's power. Otherwise, Taliban, Al Qaida will not exist and the women will enjoy more freedom.

According to our western standards, we might find it very rational. Marriages are arranged by families and love at first sight does have nothing to do with it, only respect. I would say the same situation exists in other countries than the Arab world or the Islamic religion. I've often asked this question:

"How can people with such fascinating and exuberant love poetry, content themselves with those arranged marriages?"

"Because the marriage is based on family bond, intellect, respect and social agreement."

"Why do men have the right to polygamy and to marry 4 women if they wish to?"

"For two reasons: first, in the old times, men were warriors and were dying big time. Therefore, this was a solution for widows and orphans to find another man able to protect their family and provide what was necessary. The second reason is that physiologically men have more sexual needs than women" (sexist, are you telling me? To be honest, I would be really bothered if I had to satisfy four husbands). *And last but not least, we are authorized to take four wives only if we can treat them equally. So, you need a lot of energy and financial resources, otherwise stand aside."*

Besides, nowadays polygamy is starting to decline.

When I arrived, I was horrified by their approach, without feeling, to a love affair. We have to admit, that in the west we are imbued with stories about passion in love, monogamy (except certain Mormons!), mates who complete each other and so on. It is one of the best scoops in the media business, like the latest diet; love is a strong and interesting theme which brings huge revenues. Only love between two human beings, because if we overlook universal love, it's not trendy enough and we can't take it to the bank. We easily forget the number of marriages which end in sordid divorces, with pathetic lawsuits, where children are hostages of the strife. That's obvious; we love each other so much... and money!

CHAPTER 7

Islam: some notions

THERE ARE THREE BRANCHES of Islam: Sunni, Shiite and Sufi. Muslims can believe in another form of Islam, as the Druzes and the Ismailias. The differences between these branches are meaningful and are the cause of brutal conflict.

For the Sunnis, there is only one true doctrine: Allah and his prophet Mohammed and the Holy Koran.

The schism between the Sunnis and the Shiites occurred when Mohammed died. The Shiite's belief is based on the Imam system. After Mohammed's death, there could not be another prophet, but a leader for the Muslims called Imam (the first one was Ali, one of the Mohammed's relatives). This Imam was directly named by Allah; like the Prophet, he was entitled to communicate directly with Allah. The Imam might bear a family connection to Mohammed. Those Imams were sinless and might be followed and obeyed as was Mohammed. The Shiites believe that only twelve Imams were designated by Allah. Already eleven Imams have lived. The Shiites are waiting for the 12th, the last one, who is supposed to come to earth only for "Armageddon".

The Sufis are considered to be the mystic branch of Islam. It's an esoteric attitude (*batin*) for the inner concept of Islam. Its doctrine is a spiritual interpretation of the Koran. The Sufis are the contemplatives of the Islamic revelation. It's from this point that the Sufis' exegesis of the Koran begins, determining the facts around Mohammed's words, as every word would have several interpretations, every letter its own meaning and every definition involves a path toward spiritual growth (*Matha'*).

As for the Druzes, they believe in unity and are waiting for the return of "Madhi". They are far the most conservative, and their Holy book is kept hidden. The content can only be revealed to men who are more than 40 years old and who have proved their total faith.

In summary, the Sufis are the most conservative then the Shiites and finally the Sunnis. The Druzes are not considered to be Muslims by the other three branches.

As said, everything depends on the interpretation of the Koran and the Hadith: women, marriage, family, inheritance, share of the assets and tolerance.

Today, Islam is one of the biggest monotheist religions after Christianity (more or less one billion of Muslims). The spread of Islam has been extremely fast; in one century it was pouring out of Spain to China.

Islam is, at the same time, a religion and a way of life. For Muslims, Islam is a framework for both life and society. It is a religion which advocates peace, compassion and forgiveness. Yes, indeed! In this religion, there is no partition between the real world and spirituality. Any human being should adopt the right attitude as defined in the Koran and the Hadith. Some fundamental obligations are imposed upon believers. Those obligations are known as the five Pillars of Islam.

-Profession of faith (*shaada*): to only accept belief in one God (Allah) and his prophet (Mohammed).

-Prayer (*salat*): those prayers occur 5 times a day (dawn, noon, afternoon, dusk, night)

-Charity (*zakat*): every Muslim must contribute to some charities (about 5% of their non invested assets).

-Fasting (*Ramadan*): during the month of Ramadan, you are not allowed to drink, eat, smoke, or have sexual intercourse from dawn to dusk. Each year, the month of Ramadan falls differently on our Gregorian calendar. Ramadan commemorates the date where the content of the Koran was revealed and the victory of Mohammed's followers at the Badr battle. The celebration on the end of Ramadan (*Eid*) begins with a special prayer and a lot of family gatherings.

-Pilgrimage (*Hajj*): Every good Muslim must go at least once to Mecca, according of course to his means and his health.

Muslims perceive their religion as a part of their daily routine. There is no distinction between what is sacred, what is tradition, what are moral values, laws and political affairs. The Koran, by the way, states the economic rules denouncing profits gained from usury and gambling. It also establishes the principles of justice according to the Sh'aria law. Generally, Islamic heritage is deeply anchored in people's minds. Islamic customs govern the social and professional life. Special care must be taken to how to dress, speak and behave.

The family's role

The scale of Muslim values is as follows: religion, family, tribe and lastly friend. The Koran is clear on the meaning and duties that parents should take into consideration. The husband/father's role as a provider and a protector, the wife/mother's role as a hostess and guardian of the children, are obvious. As I mentioned above, marriages between extended families or within tribes have been traditionally preferred, which lead to those arranged weddings. This fact, added to the ability to have up to 4 wives has contributed to a very large extension of family size. Often, several generations live under one roof.

Women

The Islamic Arabs are raised according to Islam rites, like Western women who are educated in the Christian, or Judaism standard. In the seventies, the feminism helped us a lot in achieving freedom; not so long ago, we could not vote! Although, we succeeded in gaining this freedom, it's still the case in some western countries that for the same job or level of responsibility, we are not paid the same salary and there is always couple's battery. I can't wait to see more female presidents!

In Arab countries, except Afghanistan, Saudi Arabia, the women have the choice to cover themselves or not, and if only few of them work, it's because they still prefer to prioritize their family life. Nowadays, more and more are going to university and are becoming highly educated. Among my in-law's family, some are covered, some are not and for working, it's the same. Contrary to western belief, women are a true asset to their environment. They play an essential role in the family and are the real leaders inside their little realm. Very often, the nasty comments I got, because I was European and acting in a certain way, came from women rather than from men. They are very eager to transmit Muslim principles to their kids. The results of their actions are evolving slowly but surely, considering than in the UAE, Kuwait, Bahrain and elsewhere, the question is how to include them in the government. There is still some improvement to be made, but we're almost there, we must allow a bit more time.

I've lived in USA in a gated community where 70% of the people were Jewish. I could observe the different rites of this religion. The orthodox side is the most conservative branch. Women wear wig or a scarf to hide their hair, they only dress with long skirts and long sleeved shirts (it's almost the same rule than in the Muslim dress code). When they have their period, they must sleep in another room and they are not allowed to touch food, as they are considered to be impure. As a woman, one day I was told not to touch a religious man, even if he was asking for my pen! I never encountered that in the Arab world. Finally, the kosher culinary customs are not that easy to follow and are more difficult than

Halal rules. Each of us is raised according to some more or less rigid conventions, so that we should not judge others too harshly. I moved out of this community, because as an agnostic I had to bare some discrimination, above all on the Shabbat day, where, sorry for that, I was driving...

Chapter 8

Notes on working conditions

The first two years were years about observation and surprise. What I liked best was seeing my kid adapt herself more and more to this new environment. After six months, she was able to speak English and she was learning Arabic with a lot of interest. She was starting to read it and to write it. She was so happy to go to the desert and, she did not have any problem making friends from different nationalities. Her awareness was stronger every day. I did not have any fear for her because the crime rate was almost zero (of course, it did rise when the population increased, but, still the UAE are quite safe). I did not lock my car or my house. I never had any problem, except one time: while we were asleep at night, a teen came into my home through the unlocked window and stole some cash from my wallet. He had the courtesy to put the wallet back in my purse!!

But some emotional matters got entwined with some sensitive professional situations.

As I wrote previously, I was hired by a Greek-Saudi family to manage a small company. I spent a lot of time setting up a stock management and accounting PC program while I was supervising the stores as well. After a year and a half, six stores were opened in the Middle East and I was quite happy with the results. Until the day where "Big Boss" tried to explain to me that in spite of my good work, my salary was too high for the company, and it would be better if I could find another job. Before leaving it would be nice if I could train a secretary (!!!!) so she would be able to continue the job, by the way, I was very pretty but without any charisma and the friendship established with each other became null and void. Bang, bang, bang!

Fortunately, at this time the country opened its doors to foreign investors to set up new companies, so I found another job pretty quickly, better paid but definitively weirder.

This time, it was not unscrupulous slave drivers but obviously some psychopathic crooks. They decided to invest in Dubai, dragging with them as a burden, their useless son and daughter in law. At the beginning, they hired the top notch people from finance and management. I was the executive assistant of the chairman/owner. The interview I had with "Madame" first, and with "Sir" was an omen of having crazy days.

"Madame" was convinced she looked like Marylin Monroe. The only snag was her cross eyes (this explains, perhaps, the mistaken image reflected in her mirror) and intellectually, she was as clever as Madeleine Albright. Their two I.Q were not measured in the same institute, I guess.

"Sir" with Ray Ban sunglasses and his haircut, had the look of an aging Elvis Presley, but he thought he was Marlon Brando's clone (although… at the end of his life, I would say why not?).

I was lucky enough to have some "out of this world" conversations with these two clowns.

"Madame" telling me that her little strabismus problem was due to the fact her left brain was too powerful! In order to correct this imbalance, her physician had recommended, when she was a kid, some exercises to develop her right brain. Soon, the poor girl had to stop, because her right brain started to become too overpowering! Please, don't dare to smile or laugh, just take a deep breath and show some compassion, excuse yourself for going to the restrooms and there burst in laugh.

"Sir", (great moment also) was recounting the miraculous story of his encounters in Africa, a story which could have been the biggest drama in his life. Just imagine, his two daughters were swimming too close to the coral barrier without realizing the danger, when the waves started to pull them away and swallow them up. What to do?? The current and the waves were too strong for him to help them. So, abracadabra…he called on God for assistance, and suddenly, miraculously, the waters parted in front of him, and in a great jump he went to rescue them: safe and sound. Doesn't it remind you the story of Moses? It's much better than Zorro or Lucky Luke!

The game did not last a long time, because insanity and business are not meant to match. We were laid off one after another, the debts were piling up, and the owners were not committed to paying what they owed. So, when the couple left the country, leaving their son behind, he and his wife decided to ask the Indian coffee boy, who did not know how to write or read English, to sign a document stating he was in charge and financially responsible for the company. The poor boy believed he was signing a paper to obtain his passport, but instead he was caught and sent to jail when the suppliers and the sponsor took legal action against the company for nonpayment.

I contacted all the people I knew including a lawyer who was able to take the case and get "Little Indian" freed, as well as to obtain the seizure of the son and daughter in law's passports (still living in Dubai).

You have to keep in mind that you can get a residence visa, only if you work for a company which will sponsor you, if you are an investor or if you are a spouse (minimum income is required in that case). The visa is valid for 2 years now, and can be renewed and paid if all the conditions are fulfilled. The major drawback to getting a residence visa through company sponsorship is that, if you decide to quit your job or if you are fired, this company has the right to impose a six month's work ban, which prevents you from finding another position. So here I am, without a job, in the middle of July 1995. I chose to go to France to see my family and rest a little bit, after such turmoil. I was able to stay all summer, where the weather was much better and I came back at the end of August.

Let me describe the situation: no work, no unemployment benefits, I needed to use my savings, because the professional segment where I worked was hard to crack. But still, I had to raise and take care of my daughter, to pay my rent and bills, so I started to freak out, and rather than remain with nothing, I took the opportunity to work at the French school as a substitute for the elementary class for one month, then I took a shift as a nurse (thanks to have studied medicine before business). Happily, I found a job in November which was more interesting but not very well paid. I would have to wait for a year and a half before being contacted by a headhunter.

My boat was feeling the wind again; sometimes this wind blows a bit hard...

After several interviews, I got a job from again a Saudi company. It reminded me a kind of merry-go-round where the kids have to grab the toy waved by a guy. Finally, I was able to get another business development manager position, with a good salary and an attractive expat package: medical insurance for my daughter and me, her school fees paid, financial compensation for my house and car, plus a return ticket to France for both of us.

Far from easy, it was a challenging position. I had under my supervision six stores established in the UAE; I had to find effective solutions for turning their losses into profits and for converting the colossal dead stock in the warehouse into cash. My boss was living in Saudi Arabia and did not have the same sense of humor as me, or the same business vision. After several conflicts quite tough, we became good colleagues and then friends.

The employees from luxury outlets are true caricatures which regale my cynical sense of humor. They are The Brand. They live, eat, sleep and get laid according to the brand's criteria. They feel chosen and watch the rest of the world with contempt, except of course, the fashionable and wealthy "aficionados", who have the means to display some good labels behind their back, just to show which social class they belong to.

I kept the best for the end of this satire: two merchandisers from Agnes B! Hilarious but extremely unnerving; I was really ready to make them eat their silk paper. One entire day to arrange two small display windows! AAAAAAHHHH! Please, give me some Xanax; they spent the rest of the day congratulating each other.

Anecdote: an Emirati woman entered the Dior boutique and used her *abaya* to steal a bag *(burqa* and *abaya* are not always a disgrace!). The confrontation was quite interesting! To open the woman's *abaya* and call the security guard was really amusing. It's not because you have some money that you should pay, is it?

Another great moment that I recall was the grand opening of Ines de la Fressange's boutique. I was able to arrange a phenomenal opening in one of the best place in Dubai, with fashion show and live band. Forget the humility, it was superb; the French Ambassador and 300 guests were completely enchanted.

This memory is triggering another festive and entertaining event which took place later, when I joined Cartier in 2000: the polo match we organized between Cartier and a local team. A moment of great happiness and pride to see the best polo's players and all the "Jet Set" well dressed, rushing forward to be the chosen guests (I am a bit snobbish but I know how to use self derision in order to not be fooled by this kind of environment). The only similar event you can find is the Equestrian World Cup race of Dubai. The show is not only in the field with the best racing horses ever but also, inside the stands. Be compassionate, as wearing hats with feathers or other beads when it's so hot, could be worthy of respect and even admiration.

Finally, one more inconvenience in this country is the justice system. As I already wrote, the Middle East is governed by the Sh'aria law, so it's not at all the same reference we know in western countries. This justice is partial toward foreigners. There are irritating levels of discrimination and the judges look like more caravan drivers than men defending the law.

First, racial discrimination: European people are more favored than Asian people, then social discrimination related to the professional position you have, and who you know, and finally sexual discrimination.

You have to understand that construction laborers and maids are mainly hired in India, Sri Lanka, Pakistan, Philippines and now China. These people immigrate to the UAE because the conditions of life are harsh in their home countries. They think that here, they can find a better way to survive decently and take care of the rest of their family. Most of them come from a very poor environment. At the beginning, it is very disarming; their common sense is so different. Example: an Indian pedestrian who has crossed 2/3 of a street, then sees a car coming, instead of running forward in order to reach the other side, will turn back?! They arrive in what they dreamed to be an "El Dorado" and are treated more like cattle than human beings. The only thing they can aspire to, are a roof (but they are rough-stacked), some food, some clothes and a small amount of money to send to their family remaining home in misery.

A laborer earns 1,500 AED per month (410 USD), the same for maids, gardeners, drivers and waiters. It seems that slavery is not abolished in this country: low salary, working conditions very hard, residence visa granted only if the employer is willing to do so, passport confiscated by the employer, no unemployment benefits, no union and almost no way to sue your boss for grievances. In the UAE, any expatriate can be fired on the spot with a very small or no compensation. I know pretty well about that!

On the other hand, when I questioned several people on this matter, everybody was explaining to me that in spite of the tough working conditions, they were relieved to provide new financial support for their kids and their parents, so they can eat, drink what they need. It's quite difficult to imagine such a situation for us who are spoiled. I almost forgot to mention that in UAE, you have to work overtime and if, unfortunately you work outside, the work will stop only if it is more than 140oF. I just can picture a nice European or Western crew laying asphalt in the middle of the summer, above all if it's the month of Ramadan!

When I visited India and the Philippines, I could understand better what they were telling me in Dubai. The misery over there is hardly bearable. Entire families live in the streets, staying on and under plastic bags and boxes, surrounded by wandering animals. The rivers are used as bathtubs, washing machines, dish-washers and garbage bins. How can we have this huge gap between the West and the third world countries?

Other jobs are better paid for the Westerners, because we benefit from our expatriate status. We normally take care of our own health insurance and retirement because we don't pay any income tax. Yep! Not everything is bad.

We experienced true happiness alongside those humble people. As Westerners full of concepts of human rights, respect and freedom, we had, I guess, a different approach than the Bedouins. The fact that we considered them as human beings and not like cattle led us to develop a privileged relation with them and learn true kindness. I still feel nostalgic about Nirupa, who was our maid for so many years. She was amazing, refusing to rest as long as the house was not spic and span, the dinner ready and the dishes washed. She never forgot my daughter's birthday or New Year. Naweed, the driver who took back and forth Camille for school, considered her as a member of his own family. Vijay, our stable boy who took care of the horses, is still writing some letters to me full of empathy and kindness.

Those people touched me and taught me a side of life which I did not know before. I have a great respect for their humility, kindness and the wisdom that comes from sharing.

And then, there were the mean, unscrupulous, vicious ones, the crooks and the new slave traders...

CHAPTER 9

Discussion about values

THE MIDDLE EAST'S MIRAGE and the "El Dorado" dream have led and still lead people to unbelievable actions. Those sharks arrive, in what they consider their occupied territory, and do not give a damn about learning the Arab culture, the tradition or the religion. The West has an arrogant tendency to consider Arab people as slow-witted and still living, until recently, in the middle of the desert with their herds of goats and camels. That's a mistaken perception of what motivates the heart of each of them. In barely 40 years they shifted from the sand to skyscrapers! At first encounter, they are respectful of the family's values, they are able to be welcoming and generous, but be careful if you cheat them or betray their honor. Those men and women who know how to open their hearts will become furious and cruel warriors, ready to die to save their honor and their beliefs. Nothing will stop their fight and their revenge.

First lesson to keep in mind: don't mix them up; Arabs are from the Middle East and have nothing to do with Persians and North Africans. They don't even speak the same dialect, and to understand each other they have to use classic Arabic. Their food is slightly different as well as their traditions and their political and economical expectations. They only share the same religion with the differences I mentioned before. I went to Morocco, Algeria, Egypt, Lebanon, Jordan, of course the UAE, but also Bahrain, Qatar and Oman; I met a lot of Saudi Arabians, Kuwaitis, Syrians, Pakistanis, Yemenis, Iraqis, Iranians and Afghans; when I spoke with them, I had to adapt my views on the countries from the Gulf and their neighbors.

Over there, the conflict between Israelis and Palestinians is a difficult topic because it's not a politically correct discussion (even for the West). The analysis of the Hebrew state leads immediately to an anti-Semitic frame of reference. There are many anti-Semitic people throughout the world; we must fight them as we must fight any racism without creating a new form of discrimination, and try to reach the goal of quelling negative discourses about Arabs and Israel. Proof of historical facts is available: there was a lot of suffering for the Jewish people: Pogroms, Shoah, Nazi camps (some members of my family went to those camps or were hidden during the war) but it will never justify in my mind, the banning of criticisms (often positive) concerning them. What about genocides of Kurds, Armenians, South Africans, Rwanda, Chinese and so and so. Why the Jewish community forbade the Romanis to have also a celebration spot in Berlin? My approach is the same regarding Europeans, Americans, Arabs or whomever.

The Israeli homeland is built upon the land of others (which is tragic for them as well as for the Arabs), and their government, encouraged by the American one, destroys all the hopes for peace that the Israeli people deserve. When George W. Bush accepted Israel's retention of its settlement in the Palestinian territory, he advanced the murder of Israelis as well as Palestinians. The Arab world has difficulties in recognizing that the Jews have the right to get this land. They disagree that these people can own a land just because it was God's promise. They require some real proof of this "promise". They believe that this territory belongs to them and that the partition following the 1948 agreement is an arbitrary action for an invasion without any compensation and a manipulative act contrived by the West, in order to divide the Arab world and to keep some control. Consequently, they don't recognize

Israel as a country, even to the extent that on the geography books or maps in the Arab schools, Israel does not exist and you can't see its name.

To the layman, as I wrote in the preface, I did not graduate from any geo-political or economic institutions. That said, this does not prevent me from having certain thoughts and perceptions about a situation I find to be deplorable. I think that Israel does not play a fair game and does not take appropriate measures for obtaining peace and understanding between two peoples, who have a lot in common, whatever we may think. The latest proof of the Israeli despotism: the Supreme Court of Justice has just decided that mixed couples (Israeli-Palestinian) can no longer live in Israel!!! Therefore, hundreds of Israeli civilians of Arab origin are prohibited from staying with their Palestinian spouse in Israel. Doesn't it remind you something?

What bothered me most is the biased attitude from the rest of the world regarding this conflict, which has last for so many years. For sure, it serves some interest…When Israel attacks the Palestinians with extremely sophisticated weaponry (air force, missiles and tanks against rifles, machine guns and stones) we say that it's legitimate for them to protect their territory and people; but when the Palestinians try to protect their land bombing with mortars where they can, we call that terrorism! From which the following slogan: "Resisting is not terrorism", according to the Arabs, and as for "War on terrorism" in the West, something even better, as Mr Bush said: "If you are not with me, you are against me". From both sides, innocent civilians die, but certainly more on the Palestinian side than the Israeli one. Since when should a war be clean?

In 1982 the worse act of terrorism in the History of the Arab World occurred, when the Flanges allies and Israel orchestrated three days of rape, torture and murder in the Palestinian camps of Sabra and Chatila. This massacre was followed by Israel's invasion in Lebanon, in order to eliminate the PLO. This operation was hacked by the US Secretary of

States, Alexander Haig. The death of more than 17,000 Palestinian and Lebanese civilians was reported. The truth has to be told.

As for the Arab world, it persists in an intolerance which generates blind violence. The repetition of terrorist acts undermines the basis of Islam, which calls for peace and the respect of others. Those actions are, obviously, a mean to show the entire world the different standards and the unfair prejudices they have to deal with. This situation and the means used serve only to widen the huge gap between the East and the West. A small extremist group cast a slur on the Muslim religion, as well as the Zionists who worsen a crisis which is already at the breaking point, and draw a picture of Judaism as a totalitarian and fundamentalist religion. The religion collide with one another, forgetting the innocents, who are moderate and would prefer the peace of mind of seeing their children grow up in joyful and carefree surroundings.

What a lot of tragedy, massacre and hate for the sake of religions which promote love, tolerance and respect. I must add that the worst barbaric acts were done by Christians and Muslims. Even if now Israel scares people with its influence and power, before that, Jews were wiser. It took only few lunatic and fundamentalist individuals to damage what could have been a quiet compromise. How far in our excessiveness and decadence should we go, so that we reach a real consciousness? God and nature will be forced to have the last word. In this apocalypse, our regrets, our tears and our blood will not change anything. We evolve technologically, but we stagnate in our humane idiocy. Or perhaps, religion has nothing to do with that, perhaps only ego, power and greed are the common factor.

I am a bit puzzled with what's going on in Europe. Suddenly, after years of living far from their homeland, Muslims get the need to show some obvious signs of their religion. We see covered women, prayer in the streets and so on. Should we see means to fight against discrimination, ghettos, bad integration? Do we ask the right question to answer to this situation properly? I doubt so.

CHAPTER 10

Arab world's differentiation

I KNOW THE ARABS, having lived with them a part of my life and this turmoil makes me suffer deeply. It sullies my memories of pleasure, fun and life. I spent a splendid period of my life in Dubai. I had to prove myself professionally and socially, but I have always been supported, helped, motivated, loved and respected.

After some disappointments, I established an effective style of communication and I became a respected speaker. Honestly, in the beginning, it was hard to talk about contracts, finances and commercial strategy, when you know that the business world is largely controlled by men.

We must keep in mind that each Middle East country has its own customs and point of reference, even though they share the same geographic area. There is not really a consensus among them. To be united is a real challenge but they have to come to this point if they want to stay in the world picture.

For instance, Saudi Arabia is overwhelmed and spoiled by its oil production (although a minority is wealthy, the rest being pretty poor), consequently, it made many compromises with the USA which protect for the moment the royal family. Saudi Arabia is also controlled by a religious supremacy. There are millions of pilgrims who come to

Mecca to pray at the *Kaaba*. So underlying, there is a conflict between technological evolution combined with some money and political agreement, and Islam's fundamentalist principles. As a result, it has emerged a behavioral unrest, which leads to a flagrant hypocrisy and a rather disconcerting interpretation of the Koran.

In Saudi Arabia the women must wear *abaya* (Muslim or not) and *shila*. Don't try to disobey because the ever-present religious police will intervene, and the *Muttawas* armed with sticks will make sure that you are aware of your infringement. You can find them again in planes going to the West, drinking gently but surely. It's the same story with Saudi women, black ghosts who are showing their mini-skirts, jeans and low-neck outfits as soon as the plane has left the Saudi territory. I saw some of them in night clubs who would embarrass Eros. Once you are in Saudi Arabia, everybody just act straight. The women not only have to be dressed up according to the religious rules (as it is in Iran and Afghanistan), but they are also not allowed to drive, hardly to work, or to go out alone by themselves. They must be accompanied by a guardian (husband, brother, member of the family or even their driver). The only jobs they can get are teaching girls, nurses or eventually sales associates for women's items.

Of course there are not movie theaters, bars, or night-clubs, so everyone has a TV connected to different satellites; it's a very profitable market. Women can travel to foreign countries but only with a written approval from their husband, brother or father. It's just a little bit better than in Afghanistan, where the goats are more valuable than women. True story: a friend of mine saw on the highway, a big white Mercedes, with two guys in the front, three goats seated on the rear seat and the two women in the opened trunk! That's nice, no?

In Saudi Arabia, the shops are opened from 10 am to 10 pm but, everything is closing during prayer time. The restaurants are divided in two: one side for men only, the other side for families (by the way, try to eat and drink when you're completely covered. It's fun and entertaining!)

Expatriates live in compounds, where inside you can do whatever you want. There are swimming pool, some shops, restaurants and fitness rooms. The people who live there make dinner and have barbecue parties. Some of them try to make wine (the taste is a bit weird) just to overcome the frustration of a non alcoholic country. By a large majority, Saudis are very frustrated by those prohibitions and this lack of freedom; so who says it's forbidden to awake the desire to overcome the interdictions, and it's quite interesting to see some ludicrous situations when they travel abroad.

At the opposite point, Lebanon because of its geographical location, has always been exposed to a multitude of international traffic and, this influence has put it at the top of the scale of liberality; moreover the high percentage of Christians has played a primary role. Lebanon is a mixture of European and Arab atmosphere combined with hospitality and joy of life.

I went there several times to see some friends or my in-laws. The first time, Beirut was still upside down and I was upset to see all the bullet and mortar holes on the building walls. There still were tanks and checkpoints on the roads, soldiers carrying rifles and machine guns. It was quite disturbing to see people suffering economically from the war. The way of life was expensive, while the salaries were very low. In fact, only 10% could afford to live comfortably and to maintain the country. There were Palestinian camps and, in 1995 they were still living in pathetic conditions. It looked like the worse slum ever, because some of the shelters were just a kind of tent made with plastic bags and cardboard. I did understand the grudge they were holding; suddenly they were lacking the primary decency of a human being: roof, food and water.

The Palestinian people are angry and they shout for their right to live with dignity, farm their land and to provide an education for their children. Time will be needed in order to suppress anger as the only motivation of their thinking, a lot of conviction and help from the West to reach a negotiable compromise.

Seeing the latest policies from Europe and the USA, I doubt this can be achieved in the short term. The Middle East is a powder keg which blazes up more and more. I hope people will handle properly their future to finally find peace on earth, which should be so beautiful. Iraq is an epiphenomenon which destabilizes this area. Arabs don't trust the West any longer. Economically, they are tied up with their trade arrangements, but emotionally the bitterness is increasing. We have to face the fact that we took advantage of them, and now the game is reversed. On this subject, I would like to quote a passage of Robert Fisk's book, which summarizes very well the state of mind in the Arab world:

"However one approaches this Arab sense of humiliation —whether we regard it as a form of self pity or a fully justified response to injustice- it is nonetheless real. The Arabs were among the first scientists at the start of the second millennium, while then crusaders (…) were riding in technological ignorance into the Muslim world. So while in the past few decades our popular conception of the Arabs vaguely embraced an oil-rich, venal and largely backward people, awaiting our annual handouts and their virgins in heaven, many of them were asking pertinent questions about their past and their future, about religion and science, about how God and technology might be part of the same universe. No such long-term questions for us. We just went on supporting our Muslim dictators around the world —especially in the Middle East- in return for their friendship and our false promises to rectify injustice.

We allowed our dictators to snuff out their socialist and communist parties; we left their population little place to exercise their political opposition except through religion. We went in for demonization —Messrs Khomeini,

Abu Nidal, Khadafy, Arafat, Saddam, Bin Laden- rather than historical questioning. And we made more promises.

Presidents Carter and Reagan made pledges to the Afghan mujahedin: fight the Russians and we will help you. We would assist the recovery of the Afghan economy. A rebuilding of the country, even –this from innocent Jimmy Carter- "democracy", not a concept to be sure that we would now be bequeathing to the Pakistanis, Uzbeks or Saudis. Of course, once the Russians were gone in 1989, there was no economic assistance.

Tell Muslims what they want to hear, promise them what they want, anything, as long as we can get our armadas into the air in our latest "war against evil".

For a long time, Africa has been attractive territory to colonize. We dried up this continent's resources without worrying about the local people who now have to face tribal wars, poverty and sickness. We were especially talented in ruining and corrupting the system, while in the meantime denouncing tribal rivalries, without bringing long-term solutions or any viable education. In order to keep a clear conscience, some countries have opened their borders, but without any desire to integrate those people. The black people have been abused and we'd like to be thanked by them: quite amazing this lack of common sense!

Nowadays, helped by the media propaganda, some governments would like to establish democracy throughout the entire world, with no knowledge of whether the people of those countries are ready for such a system.

What sets me off is that the need to establish democracy is ultra selective and is inexplicably directed to the Middle East! Why? Is there not some interest here in economically and politically controlling these lands, and some means of self enrichment (G.W. Bush, Cheney, and so on...)?

It's quite odd that Cuba, Korea, china etc... arouse only minor interest.

At the present time, Machiavelli would seem a cute toddler when faced with the scale of today's manipulation.

Let's continue to meditate on the Holocaust, a human tragedy that's hardly bearable (the stories I've heard in my family still give me goose pimples) but we must also keep in mind: The Inquisition, slavery, massacre of the Native American Indians, Kurdish and Armenian genocides, millions of people killed under Stalin's and Mao's regimes. Tortures suffered while Castro and Pinochet governed their country, Algeria, South Africa, Iran, Iraq and so many other places. The list of atrocities between human beings is so long.

We're shocked by Islam's hypocrisy, because it exists, but honestly, do we do better? Under the guise of religion, democracy and freedom, we are doing awful things. Is God happy with our hate and intolerance? I suppose He did the best He could when He gave us the choice.

The most astonishing when I question some people is that most of the time, the most definitive judgments come from those who have rarely traveled abroad, and do not have the slightest experience or cultural background to understand the Arab world. The power of prejudice and fear is so strong.

CHAPTER 11

Experiences and anecdotes.

I

N DUBAI, I ENJOYED and took advantage of a quality of life I could not have found in France. Not very funny to be a working single mother who has to find a good nanny, a cleaning lady, to pay her rent, insurance, income tax and whatever else. I preferred to go far from my roots and raise my daughter comfortably. Because I had people to help me at home, I could spend my free time with Camille. We discovered other surroundings, we talked a lot, we had fun together and we could enjoy some shared activities. We traveled to Egypt, Africa and Asia. We became passionate about horses and the horse whisperer's method. We followed several endurance horse races through the dunes. We learned so much from the nature. I discovered Martial Arts through an amazing Master who taught me the discipline of body and mind. He made me better. I worked also with a "spiritual mentor". She opened my eyes and my spirit to another dimension and another kind of acceptance. A *little English Lady,* who is very dear to my heart.

That said, our life was not free of dramas. We had to cope with the loss of two of our beloved ones: my mother and Camille's father. Obviously, this country where we could nest and feel safe helped us overcome our sorrows. We could adjust and regain our balance because the ambiance was pleasant and mellow. We received a lot from some friends and I'm not sure I would have got the same somewhere else. We could also set free our love for animals, especially horses and cats. I met Mouhiddine in Dubai, and at first sight, I knew it would be joyful. Our local marriage was a joke. I was 40 and I had to provide a letter from my father to approve the wedding (from my Jewish side, my father asked me, when I was young, never to marry an Arab and now he loved my husband as his son!!! Unbearable lightness of human being…), also I had to fill a form as I was a virgin!!

Our free time was filled with affection and positive energy. I could practice Martial Arts with an extraordinary Master, ride horses in the middle of the dunes, fully enjoying the sunset and the silence, and grow spiritually with a genuine mentor. It's only because of those moments of such bewilderment that we could stand the harshness of this people.

They have a quite low level of sentimental feelings as we understand them. The Arab people live in an arid land, with weather that sometimes reaches a paroxysm. In summer, temperatures can peak at 130o-140oF, with 90% humidity; it's physically very hard. At this time, the sea is very warm, about 92o-93oF and the swimming pools are cooled to keep them at 80oF; otherwise try to swim in your bathtub!

Every day I blessed the AC more than any technological invention. The shops, the malls, the cars and homes were an oasis of freshness. Fifty years ago AC did not exist; the Bedouins had no electronic appliances. This can help you understand their frugality with emotions. They were working hard, surviving despite these conditions and their only entertainment were stories told over a cup of tea or coffee, falcon hunting and camel races.

What surprises me most is the enchanting atmosphere emerging from this part of the world, and the contradiction between the 21st century's technology and the desire to be rooted in traditions of the past. On one side, the respect of Islam which pushes a minority of people to a fanaticism based on a mistaken interpretation of the Holy texts, which brainwashes the most underprivileged people; after all when you do not have anything to lose, the promise of Heaven with its 72 virgins, the river of honey and milk could seem a good prospect. On the other side, the will and the need to challenge the forbidden; the feeling is always more enjoyable. Most of the Muslims follow the religion's principles and the five basic pillars. Others manage the ambiguity in a more chaotic way.

Often, I saw prostitutes in hotels and bars, some local men getting drunk, verging on comatose, supporting several lovers, while being addicted to drugs. I met Saudis, Kuwaitis and Emiratis who were refined gentlemen, smart, rational during the day, but became like "Mr Hyde" at night. Most were wealthy and well educated but were raised by maids rather by their parents, so they missed some emotional development milestones concerning affection and self-esteem. When they drink they lose sights of the mental boundary, go back to their childhood and behave as naughty capricious kids. Because they think money can buy anything, they feel they are entitled to everything. So we see situations which are sometimes funny, but more often pathetic. Moral and psychological miseries are by far the worst which can happen to a human being; they lead them to be inconsistent, compulsive and phobic. It is true for any population in any country.

The main point is to use our analytical skill to try to understand why a mature man can fear the night, his loneliness and his low self-esteem. To relieve this phobia, alcohol is the best suited, as well as inviting some pseudo friends to all get stupefied together. This can lead a successful businessman to revert to his youth and to lose all logical sense. I did collect some memorable anecdotes regarding this matter.

Sheikh Ali is seated in front of his nth glasses of whisky, his cigarettes and lighter by his side, but each time he needed a cigarette, he asked his butler to light one up for him and put it in his mouth. Then, suddenly he started to mime a military march, and all the guests had to applaud his performance! He sat back and then decided to recite some poetry.

Once, one of his guests could not wait any longer to go to the restroom, so he stood up. Sheikh Ali ordered him to stay.

"Ali, please, I need to go to the toilet."

So Ali addressed his butler: "Mahmud, go and fetch the toilet."

I swear, I didn't make it up. Another time, Sheikh Ali was supposed to return home, the plane for Riyadh was at 10pm; unfortunately he already started to drink and to lose his self control. His staff hurried him to get ready to leave for the airport.

"No, the plane is leaving at midnight, I have plenty of time."

"Sorry Sheikh Ali, but the departure is at 10pm and we must go now."

"No, if Sheikh Ali says the plane is at midnight; it's at midnight."

Result: the team arrived at the airport at 11pm, in time to hear that the plane left an hour ago. Even better, the day after it was the same story, all over again. You need a good sense of humor, some detachment and a lot of patience to bear working in such an environment. At least your high salary is a very good compensation!

Another story: one day an Emir asked me if I knew a good restaurant, preferably French, where he could take his wife for dinner. As he appreciated French wine, I advised him to taste a "Bordeaux" which he did not know (Lynch Bages). The next day, I received a thank you message from the restaurant for sending this couple. Because they also drunk a "Chateau Lafitte" and were absolutely amazed by it, he bought all the remaining bottles; a little intimate dinner costing him only 10,000 USD.

This extravagant spending really irritates some people who judge it to be a waste. Instead, I see someone who has unlimited financial means, but needs reassurance and affection to soothe his insecurity. In the end, he contributes to the luxury economy and thereby to all those who work in it. How can this kind industry survive without those V.I.P's? I can easily put myself in the shoes of a cab driver or a waiter who receive a tip, worth 10% of their salary. It will ease their life to pay their bills or to buy a gift for their child. Only, I'd like to see those wealthy people helping more the needy, poor and sick ones.

CHAPTER 12

Social situations

IN FRANCE, IT'S TASTELESS to show that you are successful, you earn money and you spend it. It is politically incorrect now, to talk about a cleaner or a garbage man; you should rather say a cleaning technician. There are no more black people or half-castes, only colored people; me, I would rather be called a "tanned bidet". Where this demagoguery is leading us? It's an invitation for hypocrisy, stabbing in the back, frustration and numbing people's brains.

Our governments should be more concerned about serious situations as, why there is so much violence, overpopulation, globalization, decrease in our purchasing power, unemployment, creation of utopian needs and top notch V.I.P's who abuse financially the population. A government which is really concerned should provide to everybody three fundamental rules: Safety, Education and Health care! This negation of reality reminds me of the famous remark of the French Queen Marie-Antoinette "The people have no more bread; so let them eat cakes".

That's true, in the UAE, the social hierarchy is important but nobody is dying of starvation. Yes, there is a plethora of luxury cars, but ask the companies which manufacture them to stop their exports; I am pretty sure that the employees would be ecstatically happy to find out that the wealthy are less rich and consequently have to be laid off. Yes, it's not a democracy and the health care is not so good. I worked more than 40 hours a week keeping in mind I could be fired if my performance was not good enough. Yes, although I was wrongly laid off, I was also extremely well paid and I did not pay any income tax, just because it does not exist and the sales tax was/are only 4%. As there are no good health care or pension systems in place, no deduction are withheld from your salary. It's up to you to obtain any health or retirement plans; so at least, I am sure to get my pension for my old age.

Those facts discourage any employee from missing work because of a cold or a painful PMS episode; it stimulates the will to work, to fight, rather than to fall into hypochondria, or living on charity. I know it is not for everyone and I understand that some of us prefer to be supported by our welfare states (especially now as I have MS). In that part of the world the reality is simple and brutal; you work, you earn money and you obtain the right to stay, otherwise come here just as a tourist. The rules are very simple: you behave right and everything is fine; you don't, you go to jail and then, you are deported to your country.

And again, this contradiction between the enchanting landscape, a safe way of life, hospitality and service long forgotten in the West and, the aridity and frugality of feelings which bring us sharply back to reality. Nobody here says "No", but this does not mean it is a "Yes". More often, when we ask for something or for a meeting, the answer is invariably "Inch Allah" (God's will) or "Bukkrah" (tomorrow). It's up to you to discern what is implied. I admit this leaves one feeling unnerved, but the best solution is to just accept this concept. We are supposed to adapt ourselves to the Middle East and not vice-versa, as Western people like to believe.

Arabs talk a lot and promise even more, but again there is no obligation to follow through. However, I've seen some agreements become official just with a hand shake. The wisest course is, when you deal with Arabs, not to take anything for granted. As long as they have a financial advantage, everything is fine, otherwise beware of a breach of contract at the last minute. My question would be: is this practice only common with the Middle East? How many promises made by the West to this people have been broken?

In a business discussion, it's frowned upon to be impatient. Firstly, an appointment made for a certain time does not imply it will take place on time. If you are lucky the wait can last just one or two hours; perception of time does not have the same importance as it does for us. Worst case, your Arab partner will not show up and here the best policy is, to avoid to becoming upset. Otherwise, it would show weakness in your self control, and would not inspire confidence. It's more sensible to make another appointment and to convince your partner, that you would be very honored if the meeting could take place. Secondly, when the meeting starts, avoid talking right away about business; the best attitude, at the beginning, is to have some casual chat about family, the different entertainment you like, or whatever, while drinking the tea you are served. All this game is of crucial importance, because your Arab partner is weighing you intellectually and morally. Do not underestimate your body language; it reveals a lot of information about your intentions. Finally, after a certain time you can talk about what the meeting was arranged for, but be aware of his reaction while you're speaking. Do not be disturbed if his phone rings and he answers, or even if somebody is stopping by to have a chat. It has been their way to manage their business for many years; don't forget the importance placed on time is of minor value; if it's not today, it will be tomorrow! *Bukkrah Inch Allah…*

When a Westerner gets up, he wonders how to make his day profitable and effective, but a Middle Easterner will wonder how to make his day enjoyable. In the Middle East, the working schedule is determined by either prayers, or by the weather, or eventually by both, or other factors. Offices are generally open from 8am to 1pm and again from 4pm to 7pm (it's changing now on in order to catch with other countries), while shops in the malls welcome customers from 10am to 10pm. This time scheme is revised during the month of Ramadan. The working time is reduced on account of fasting and *Iftar*, the moment when people break their fast, at dusk; now, you can eat, drink, smoke etc… and the night then becomes very busy because people visit their relatives and friends, so there's a lot of food and drinks to share.

Generally, in the Middle East, nights are stretched until early morning and most of the time dinner is not before 9-10pm, which is why a little nap is very welcome. In Dubai the night life is very active because there are a lot of entertainment spots and, it's a good time to enjoy family or to talk about business.

I remember a decoration project which a friend and I submitted to a Sheikh in Dubai. Our competitor was a German company. So, I gave our estimate to the Sheikh's assistant:

"Patricia, I'll call you back to give you the Sheikh's comment."

"Very good. We have stipulated in the contract that the delivery time would be three months and a deposit of 50% should be made upon signing."

"What!!! 50% deposit with the order?"

"Yes, we have to order most of the items from France and they require 50% up front."

"Nobody can impose such conditions at the palace. We pay our suppliers at the completion of the work."

"I understand, dear A., but our way uses a simple principle: 50% with the order, 50% on delivery. In short, you pay, I work; you don't pay, I don't work." I said, smiling.

"It would be the first time we accept this kind of proposition!"

"I take at risk – let me know what you decide."

When I left, I knew he was upset that a woman could argue with him, and I was not very pleased with the outcome of the meeting. I felt that I jeopardized the project, but it was out of the question to financially entrust a customer, even if he was the ruler of Dubai. If he did not wish to pay our bill, I couldn't see myself suing him and winning the lawsuit; the best next step would be a one way ticket to France. After few days, the phone rang around midnight:

"Good evening Patricia, I'm calling to inform you that the Sheikh has approved your estimate. You can stop by tomorrow to pick up your check, but instead of three months, you have only thirty days to finish the job, otherwise we'll impose some penalty for late completion."

Hurray! The villa was located at Fujairah (about 2 hours drive) and I went there 2 or 3 days a week. We worked hard and late for one month, but we did it!

Chapter 13

The lure of democracy and freedom

I f the Arab people behave in their own way, it's undoubtedly because they draw from their history their right to be different. I deplore what I see and hear about the relationship between East and West. There is so much misunderstanding and ignorance.

Each one reacts according to his intolerance, mistaken beliefs, unfairness and cruelty. Some proclaim their religion, with its principles of respect and peace, then, send out terrorists in the name of this religion. Others remember the cruelty of ghettos, but torture in their jails and build walls. Then, some others swear by democracy, but are very reluctant to elect a black person without religion!!!

Democracy as it should be (the will of the people, for the people), does not exist, since in a democratic regime only a small elite governs the country. These elite is meant to be a representative sample of its people, but we know that around 45% of the people did not vote for the elect President, or did not go to the polls, or even better, voted for the other candidate. The Greeks created this system, which should have the goal of getting a more impartial representation of the people's will, but where is the real truth? Should the countries with democratic regimes be allowed to interfere in other countries where the regime is different? The individuality of a people should prevail over groups of foreign nations which think otherwise, with other traditions and educational values. Moreover, those nations should clean their own messes and focus on making sure their own people are safe and satisfied. Although the US democratic model is the first one to be established after the Greek example, this does not mean that this system is the right one to establish in the rest of the world.

There are different interpretations of democracy; Europe is based on the separation of powers between religion and state. But Americans democracy is tied up with a kind of religious dependence. In the Middle East, it's even more obvious: the ruler may be elected as the people's representative, but religion plays a powerful role.

In reference to what Halim Barakat wrote, the Arab dream is to free themselves from their deep-rooted skeptical feeling when we discuss the remodeling of their society. The Gulf War seems to have shaken the Arab conviction that they could build a bridge between dream and reality in order to get a new start. Rather than establish an era of independence, they found themselves overwhelmed by Western domination and the threat of possible fragmentation.

Most discouraging is that Arabs continue to struggle with the same old dilemmas, now with everything exacerbated by a greater degree of dependence and by the marginalization of revolutionary change. After the Gulf War, while some felt a loss, others were happy with the victory over their old enemies. As a consequence there was a collapse of the Arab consensus on the basic principles. The collaboration needed to resolve this uneasiness seems more and more complicated and doubtful.

A report issued in 1991, during a national conference of Arab intellectuals, notes the absence of democratic life and the violation of human rights in Arab countries, as well as Western hegemony and the desire to destroy Arab abilities. It also condemns Arab rulers for monopolizing political decisions (just look what is going on now). One Arab wrote: *Because we have oil, we are losing control of our destiny. Bloodshed becomes legitimate. They take the oil from our soil and bury our hopes. Is there any future we can dream about? How many disasters must we face before finding our way? For how long will Arab governments contain the anger of their people? A viable democracy cannot be attained without overturning political alienation and the freeing of society from the State's grasp. Arabs must work for social liberation, the proper use of the economic resources, and reasonable economic development, without forgetting about building good relationships among the different tribes and Islamic sects.* In 1920, the Times quoted: "How long do we have to sacrifice precious lives in the vain intent to impose upon the Arab world a complex and expensive government they did not ask for and they did not want?"

They are able to change their regime and prepare a major revolution if they want to, but let them take the initiative, let them organize their history, let them free to choose.

The West like the East embraces a fundamental flaw in believing that their truth is universal. Why do we want to take God's place? To have a spiritual philosophy, admit to belonging to the Whole, that's one thing, but even if everyone finds his own divine sparkle, this does not give us the right to make subjective judgments. Religion has been created by human being so that rituals allow control over mankind, and until today, this serves more to kill each other than to love.

A measure of irony helps us keep in mind a certain relativity about life, and a sense of humor let us approach it joyfully. That said, such derision, the way of making fun of everything should not overtake our respect for others. We make great utterance such as "we are free until we interfere with someone else's freedom", "Don't do anything wrong to another that you would not wish to experience yourself", or Voltaire's remark: "I disagree with you, but I'll do anything to preserve your right to express yourself".

Despite being agnostic, because religious rituals are too restrictive and childish to me (don't do this, don't do that; hard to be a human being.

That must be the reason why some people are going every week to their "religious place" and then, during the week, are the worst human beings ever seen), I believe in a universal divine power as the source of creation. In following this conviction, I try to respect the opinion of others. The recently published cartoons of Mohammed attempted to be funny, which work fine for ten drawings, but the remaining two is, in my opinion, disrespectful toward a whole people's faith. I don't know what Christians would think if there were some drawings about Christ instead. On the other hand, I could see in the USA the reactions the movie "The Passion of Christ" (directed by Mel Gibson) aroused in the Jewish community and, the anger of Catholics when the movie "The Da Vinci Code" was screened. The controversy seems to be quite one-sided.

That said, I did not see anywhere in the Koran why images of Mohammed are forbidden, and I can admire in museums some miniatures of Muslim art. It's quite shameful that people already labeled as violent respond with hate and bombs to some drawings made by stupid cartoonist. More and more, willingly or reluctantly, we are entering an era of globalization which is moving us toward all living together under the same roof. It would be wise if we could respect each other and become less strident in our opinions.

Chapter 14

A kind of future

I AM WORRIED ABOUT this rise of hatred between people of different origins and beliefs. Why this violence? Why do we see an outbreak of racism? Why are we so angry? Do our instincts tell us to eliminate the weakest in order to survive on the earth's resources? Sometimes, I have the feeling that the minority (to which I belong) which strives for peace and alerts the world to the danger of trampling our origins, will be seen in short-term, as good to eradicate. History continues without learning from its mistakes.

I fear a real destabilization of the Arab world. The seizure of control of Palestinian authority by Hamas is a sure sign of an internal conflict. This fundamentalist movement is repeated in Iran, which not only has nuclear power, but also is entering into partnership with Syria. Iran is fixated on Iraq and supports the Shiites; a split maintained by the West where the media portray s distorted truth.

I am not convinced than it was Sunnis who destroyed the Al Asker mosque without outside help. But it convinced the world of the need to send foreign troops, to teach those barbarians to establish a viable government, even if it's a big lie about intervention. Better to be a hero who brings freedom rather than to admit there were political, financial and selfish interests at play.

If we look to the past, in the 70's and 80's the Saddam regime was armed by the USA, who offered political and economic support, enabling him to become a dictator. The US prides itself on setting up democracies in Arab countries, but in 1953 they chose to oust (with British help) the only democratic and secular government theretofore known in Iran, overthrowing Mossadegh (the Prime Minister) and enabling the Shah's return (who would rule the country during the next 25 years, with the West's acceptance of his regime's corruption and repression).

Why did the US, during this period, want democracy at home and dictatorship in foreign countries? Why does the US now want democracy over there, encouraged by its own imperialist policies? Under the banner of Iraqi democracy, a new Iraq and a violent rebellion among the Iraqis, the Americans used airborne power and infantry to shell the villages, bombarded the mosques (using the excuse that they were hiding place for weapons), and massacred innocent civilians. What will be the Iraqis' psychological reaction after the invasion; will everything be forgotten in the name of liberation? At the beginning of the war, the media were only showing tidy images, i.e. tours of Saddam's palace, enthusiastic pictures to allow G.W. Bush and Tony Blair's boasts, while the people were screaming out their pain.

Today, most of people know that Mr. Bush had planned this war a way before 9/11, that Saddam's regime has ended, that the jails and torture rooms have just changed their management; apparently the saviors have became the executioners. More than 3,000 soldiers killed versus more 35,000 Iraqis. Wake up people; does it not ring a bell in your mind?

I thought Nostradamus was a loony when he foresaw that the 3rd world war would start in the Middle East; now I am more skeptical about my opinion.

If the attack of September 11th has been perceived as a gratuitously violent act undertaken by some fanatic terrorists and, also condemned by most Muslim people, the American's invasion of Iraq was seen as a discriminatory act of colonization. Few people agreed with this intervention against the Iraqi government. The ousting of Saddam Hussein was taken to be a pretext for controlling a key Middle Eastern area and, for appropriating economic resources. Saddam was a tyrant toward his people (everybody knows that) but what about other dictators who rule their country with an iron hand? Nonetheless, how can one resist of the biggest oil production resources after the Saudi one, when the West is worried about its economic development and its raw materials?

CHAPTER 15

Knowledge fights fear

A LONG TIME BEFORE Islam, in Yemen, there was the kingdom of Sheba. This people worshipped several divinities and migrated, bit by bit, throughout the rest of the Middle East; so they settled in Saudi Arabia, Jordan, Iraq and Iran and formed several tribes.

The Kabbah, located in Mecca, was the divine stone and the representation of their divine idols. Those tribes lived very frugally and became nomads in order to escape from other clans, or to take for themselves the possessions of the weakest. At this time, each tribe had a chief who was considered to be the bravest one, which entailed that brothers would kill one another. During this turbulent time some new customs developed. The tribes needed warriors for fighting, protection or invasion, so it was quite common to bury baby girls alive, in order to prioritize the males' education and to avoid creating a burden or slowing down the tribe. The caravans were composed of camels for transportation, goats for milk and meat and nomads. The tents were easy to put up and down in case of an attack. Living in such precarious conditions, they were fast in relieving, cleaning themselves and eating. Everything was organized around the concept of vulnerability.

More than 14 centuries ago, when Mohammed, an orphan raised by a priest, who was a shepherd wanted to spread Allah's words, he encouraged the men to destroy the Kabbah's divinities, but when it was time to put the Black Stone back inside the Kabbah, he faced a conflict among the tribes. Each of them wanted the privilege of carrying the Stone. So, Mohammed told them that the Stone will be put on a sheet and, each chief would then be able to carry a piece of this sheet. So a beginning of peace process occurred among all the Arab clans. He gave the order to improve women's roles and forbade the killing of the unneeded baby girls. He defined the main role of women as education and protection of children.

Then, the history recounts that Mohammed's uncle, unconvinced of Allah's existence, decided to burry alive his 3 years old daughter. He took her into the desert and began to dig a hole. When it was ready, he dropped her inside, but at this moment the little girl looked at her father and started to remove the sand from his beard, saying that she could not let him be dirty. Then, touched by her kindness, he had the revelation of Allah's existence, and saw that his action was sacrilegious.

Islam has tried to undo the customs dating back to Sheba's realm, claiming they only arose from a lack of knowledge (Al Jahilia). Nevertheless, some of those old traditions remained imprinted in the Arab blood; without being aware of it, Arabs still show some signs of them (they eat very fast and leave once they have finishes their meal). Mass unconsciousness, perhaps, but still a reality; it would be wise for Westerners who also cling to their origins, to take this into account. What would you think if suddenly the Chinese undertook an invasive policy in our countries, insisting that the truth lies within Communism, in denial of the individual and in eating with chopsticks?

Will democracy resolve the issues of intolerance, racism and poverty? I don't know, but I doubt it when I observe some democratic countries: for example, in France, the borders were opened to a lot of foreigners, but French are still completely xenophobic and new laws are discussed to put a limitation to allow immigrants to set up in this country! Far from being against democracy, I was born in France and my roots are there, I lived in a monarchist country and I felt good. Living again in a democracy and being American citizen, I have the feeling that it's a cheat; my life is not easier now, it's just a matter of adapting yourself: take what is good and accept what is bad. In the Middle East, being a non-democratic country is not an issue; the people get used to it.

Conditioned by their history, their education and their temperament, some people evolve better with a democracy, while others are content with a monarchy or something else whether or not it represents executive power. Pleasing or not, from his origins an Arab will remain who he is, his daily routine and approach belong to him and, his way of negotiating is embedded in his genes along with his feelings. Feelings of love and affection don't have the same value as in the West; reasoning therefore, is not based on the same standards. Before Islam, it was forbidden to talk to a woman about love; some stigma remains today, and although Arab poetry about love is among the world's most refined and beautiful, it's far from evoking the same romanticism as in Europe. The fantasy and the imagination are not based on the same concept.

War strategy is based on concepts born centuries ago. In History, the West had a tradition of organizing battlefields and sea battles. We still almost have the same scheme because we invariably send the Air force to bombard some strategic targets and then, we complete the invasion with infantry. In the East, the strategy is based more on surprise, traps, guerillas and tricks, and even more, due to the fact that the fear of dying does not exist. Don't forget anybody who dies to defend his country or religion will leave eternally in Heaven, where there are rivers of milk and honey, purified women and the famous virgins. Therefore, as long as there is no fair consensus for peace in Iraq, Afghanistan and Palestine, I really think that brotherhood will be delayed for a long time. The Arabs no longer trust the West and they are right; unfortunately the ties between West and East are at the same time very strong and vulnerable.

And yet amidst this collective insanity, I see the compulsive development of Dubai. The desert is stepping back every day to allow construction of skyscrapers, shopping malls, entertainment centers and highways, which are not wide enough to accommodate the traffic. Fourteen years ago, I used to bring back from France some products which were badly missed in UAE, nowadays, everything is available and I take some items from Dubai with me when I go visiting France or when I come back home to Florida. Dubai, by itself is a microcosm of the whole world; there are more than 125 different nationalities who share this territory. This melting pot opens philistine eyes and gives an opportunity to perceive other standards of reference, other habits and other tastes. Obviously, when you go to Dubai, either you fall in love with the country or you flee this barbaric world. Here, your craziest fantasy can become true because the infinite is available.

In 1993, there was a two lanes road from Dubai to Abu Dhabi; it was an epic journey to drive to the other Emirate, especially at night. The road was hardly marked and was unlit, leaving the driver to do some risky guesswork. At this time, along with excessive speed, fatal car crashes were caused by hitting camels. Now, it's a five lane highway, well lit and fenced all the way. The number of fatal crashes is still the same but it's no longer due to collisions with camels; it is SUV's against big saloon cars. Proportionately, the UAE reach the catastrophic level of being almost number one in fatal accidents! Sad trophy! Young people's favorite game is racing where they can test their Nintendo game-playing skills, to the unimaginable extent where they pour oil on the road to make the skidding more funny! There are hundreds of outlandish stories, which unfortunately decimate the local youth.

It is quite fascinating to see the growth of this country, stretched between its traditions and the excessive and irrepressible attraction of modernity. Now, it's a mix of Manhattan, Disney World and desert. The buildings' architecture is absolutely phenomenal and innovative. The designers are thrilled to see the government's determination to make Dubai the most attractive place in the world; I have to admit they know how to do it, although some aberrations occur.

Among the weirdest project, there is a group of islands built into the sea in the shape of a palm tree. The engineers might have some fun with their calculations, mass/volume/gravity, to enable supporting this weight without the foundations collapsing. Tons of rocks and sand have been dumped into the sea in order to support these constructions. Let's hope that erosion from water, wind and currents will not undermine these patches of artificial ground.

A similar project, but even crazier, is the development of several islands representing the shape of the earth. You'll be able to see this structure from space; it will compete with the Great Wall of China (project put on hold for the time being, consequence of the financial crisis). This delusion of grandeur impressed me and that's not all: there is also the highest building in the world (Sheikh Khalifa Tower) which is about 2,625 feet high, with Dubai Mall in its basement, where you can find one of the world's largest aquariums. Here, when they don't have something, they make it! Let's add magnificent golf courses, tennis and squash courts, equestrian centers, airplane and parachute jumps, desert paragliding, nautical sports, aqua-lands, go-kart racing, not forgetting about Formula 1 race track and some desert rallies.

Everything began with the construction of a hotel standing in the sea, The Burj El Aral (seven stars, a first!). There was a helipad built 985 feet above the ground. Agassi had a tennis party up there and Tiger Wood hit the best drive ever in his career. The shape of the hotel is supposed to be a sail; the design is definitively amazing but I can't stop myself from seeing a big white cockroach. The interior design reminds me more of a whorehouse than a very luxury hotel. This is normal; I have French roots therefore a very cynical sense of humor.

Each time I come back to Dubai, the urban landscape is changing and sometimes it's hard to find familiar landmarks again. Before 2000, the urbanization was not so eccentric and, the expatriates who lived here were considered to be adventurers. Today it becomes a very trendy place to visit, where the elite put itself on display. I have a kind of nostalgia when I remember the previous years; everything was so simple and the atmosphere was friendly. We were able to establish good relationships with the Emiratis, but now it's more difficult because money has polluted people's mind.

The local people are not easy to approach; they stay within their community and greed seduces their spirit. Now negotiations are harsh, as tourists have spoiled the rules of the game. I have the feeling that kindness is giving way to the detrimental effects of materialism. The former nonchalance has become more subversive, the old people gave way to youths who did not build anything, who did not suffer and who only have in mind how to take advantage of this new economic situation. The prices rocket, real estate reaches some impressive heights, rents have doubled, even tripled, while wages are hardly going up. Therefore the joy of life doesn't exist anymore; the net is closing little by little.

When I was fired in 1995 from the company which was trading automotive spare parts, I had to face a very precarious financial situation. Suddenly, after earning 5,000 USD a month, I found myself unemployed for several months; and here as I mentioned there is no Medicare or unemployment compensation. I was obliged to accept whatever temporary jobs I could find and, finally, I got a position which was not so well paid (2,500 USD) but enabling me to pay my bills, knowing that in the UAE the rent had to be paid yearly and not monthly. Then, there was my daughter school's tuition (4,500 USD for a year) my car, the food and some miscellaneous expenses. I confess, I sweated blood and tears for a year and a half, but I was always able to keep my daughter happy (thanks to a friend who took her for lunches) and to have some fun.

Today, when I see the prices for rent, food and basic items, I really wonder how some people can survive with a monthly income of 1,500 USD>.

I strongly believe that I lived in the UAE during the right time period, because to find a good job with a good package was possible. Now, a lot of people arrive here and only find a fake El Dorado: the good period is over. People mix less; the atmosphere is more superficial and quite "show off". A privileged few benefit from elite V.I.P access, and the others do what they can to survive. Many return to their home countries because in their dream, they did not plan for a tough work schedule, volatile employment conditions, traffic jams and luxury thrown in their face. You have to be psychologically strong to resist this wild capitalist pressure. If you can overcome this disappointment, Westerners are more comfy in the sense they can now find Wal-Mart to push their cart around in.

CHAPTER 16

Little nostalgias

L IKE A BEAUTIFUL LOVE story, I wish this one would never finish, but even love stories have an end. We were living in a huge villa, built around a patio, located on an oasis which was designed as a polo field. The stables were next to our door and we could ride every day. Ecstatic moments shared with my daughter. We were on the edge of the desert and I have not yet experienced this feeling of joy and freedom.

As we were the owner's friends, we were always invited to watch polo matches. Quite often we came straight from riding, dirty and smelly, to suddenly find ourselves among dressed up ladies. So, we sat, beaming among the players, sipping mint tea: we all belonged to the same family. We were also part of a technical team for horse endurance races (the distance is between 80 and 100 miles). We left in the middle of the night to reach the tracks, located in the middle of desert. At 5.00am, all the horses were gathered in a big open stable and the excitement level had risen to the maximum. Sheikh Mohammed Al Maktoum and his team were among us, but here at dawn in the dunes, there was no need for sophisticated security systems. Just the whinnying and the pawing of those very beautiful Arabian horses, the rider's tension and then the cavalcade took off.

I just remember an anecdote: once, when we left the endurance site at night; as the road was narrow and not lit up, I was driving cautiously and quite slowly and someone was tailing me with a white Range Rover flashing his lights. I lost my self control and waved at him that he had to wait. When we reached the highway he overtook me infuriated; I recognized Sheikh Mohammed, Oooops... I remained quietly behind him praying he would not take any further action. Try to do that with a Western chief of government, I guess you'll have another story to tell.

I have a friend whom I respect and admire deeply. He is the coach for Al Maktoum's racing horses. We had the privilege to visit the Royal stables, where each horse is pampered as a "star", with its own groom, a special menu according to its needs, massages, walking, swimming pool (I almost envied them and wanted to change my status as a human being, but I could not run fast enough!). We saw him breaking a horse according to the horse's whisperer method. What a marvelous and emotional moment! The horses perceived us as predators, for two reasons: our eyes are situated on the front rather than on the side of our head and we eat meat, so we emit a particular odor which they can smell. They initially fear us and most of the time the breaking (a necessary step in order to teach the horse to accept a rider) is done violently, because we teach them by constraint to accept this predator on their back (most big cats, when they attack, jump on their back). The horse is compelled to be submissive to this technique, but psychologically its mistrust is strengthened, and in my opinion it's not the best way to establish a good relationship between man and horse.

The whisperers refer to the famous method elaborated first by Monty Roberts (The Horse Whisperer) to proceed with this step using the necessary softness and calm, preferring to convince the animal by using specific body language, that it has nothing to fear from someone sitting on its back. To be able to be part of such understanding and sympathy between human being and animal is always fascinating for me. The animals have a real intelligence more refined that we think, but still ignorance kills. A thought of Nietzsche famous writing pops into my mind: "I fear animals see us humans as one of their own, but one who has dangerously lost its animal sanity; I fear they consider us as an absurd animal, the one that laughs and cries, much like a disastrous animal".

After this brief explanation, it's not surprising to see Dubai well known for one of the most beautiful World Cup racing courses. And not just that, but also the most prestigious jockeys, the best horses, the trendiest hats. It's really interesting to watch that crowd shouting and posturing. I got a really happy moment to observe those people who are hypocritically congratulating each other. I love this live comedy, where the actors don't know anymore who they really are and completely forget the ridiculous nature of the situation. Definitively, I am impassioned and intrigued by the self-satisfaction of mankind. Our ego and vanity are the most powerful weapons.

The annoying development, nowadays, is the rides in the desert or in the mountains; the camels, the horses, the falcons even the dates are becoming the tourism "must". It's like a Disney World tour, where the guests go for a trip in the dunes just to have a taste of their high level of adrenalin, with no worries about getting lost, breaking an engine, making repairs, being hungry or thirsty. That's just cool! About one hour spent in the ochre sand, a photo stop on top on a dune, then a detour through an especially made-up camp where they can eat typical Arab food, ride a camel for 300 feet, see a falcon and admire a belly dancer (not always Arab). Moreover, they can bring back some knick-knacks bought in the souk: pashmina that are not longer real pashmina (the silk and cashmere mix is now viscose instead) because they only cost 35USD (at this price, you'd be a bit naïve to think that you've got a real one), and also a lot of fake Louis Vuitton, Dior, Chanel, Hermes accessories. Do not forget that thanks to the globalization, you can't get away from the Asian knockoffs.

By confronting this modernity, the Emiratis will soon see their desert shrink like a handkerchief and, as the Native Americans; they will end up on a reservation, visited by tourists coming to see what an Arab looks like. I am joking, but nevertheless, natural laws being what they are, we are stepping forward into radical change in the UAE, including weather, crime rate, pollution and cultural clashes. Without doubt it's part of the same script facing the Amazon or Alaska. There are so many of us living on earth that the conquest of virgin territories is inevitable, but of course we have to find some more raw materials in order to fill the pockets of our leaders.

The UAE example is very revealing. From a country where nothing was established, I now find myself facing a Megalopolis. Time is money, the sipping of coffee goes faster and faster although some traditions are preserved. Middle Easterners adapt themselves to the new rhythm, deciding they will take part in this globalization. In consequence they are losing their spontaneous spirit, their generosity and their purity. Negotiations are becoming more difficult.

Last trick in 2007: if you wanted to rent an office, first you had to be extremely patient because demand was higher than availability, and secondly, not only the landlord increased the rent by any astounding and arbitrary way imaginable, but you had to bribe the real estate agent in order to secure the location! When you told the agent that it was completely illegal, he smiled and agreed but answered that there was no law governing this matter. So you took it or left it.

Perhaps, just keep in mind the exuberance of hotels, restaurants, gold and marble. It's the tale of "the 1001 Nights" updated for the 21st century and for our frustrated collective subconscious. At lastly, when you are ready to leave, you'll be able to admire one more time the luxury shops at the airport Duty Free. In this riot of light and marble, you'll get the last glimpse of the gold souk, the spice market, the fabrics, rugs and little knick-knacks. After, really gently, use the flight time to readapt yourself psychologically to your own routine, your small two bedrooms apartment, the gloomy weather and the unfriendly faces. Maybe the nostalgia of those colors, odors and impressions of ardent life will open your mind and your heart. Happiness does not have color, religion, prejudice or fear. Happiness comes from inside and the best way to protect yourself is to open your arms to others.

Chapter 17

Hopes and doubts

WHAT'S GOING ON WITH the Arab world? In each cycle of evolution there is a transitional period that undergoes destruction and chaos. We want to compensate for what is lost, to catch the train of our destiny. Some are successful, some fail. New civilizations are born, bringing new hopes, but always leaving behind some lives torn apart and broken with tragedy. We are in a powerful transformation and mankind will adapt to new rules. It will be most difficult for those who knew the past. They will be able to compare, to evaluate the loss of their reference points; they will suffer from their mistakes and carry the burden of regret and remorse. We live in a perfect world utopia, but how could this be, emerging from our imperfection? We stick to our fairy tale vision which has nothing to do with reality.

Again, Lebanon is torn between pro and anti Syrian, Syria, Libya and Yemen want to get rid of their dictator like Tunisia and Egypt; Saudi people are not happy with the Royal family, which is seen as a clown in the pay of USA and where a lot of Saudis are poor. Kuwait has sold its soul to the liberating countries; Afghanistan switches its trust from the Taliban to the Americans; Bahrain is confronted to Shiite and Sunni cleavage; Iraq which believed in freedom but is controlled by the US regime seeking its oil supply; Iran which is ready to strike, flouting the U.N. resolutions by continuing its nuclear program in order to distract its people from their misery (Do you remember the troubles during the last election?). The Palestinians who are torn apart between the rivalry Hamas/Fatah, while Israel is enjoying this fratricidal conflict, colonizing more territories and still refusing negotiating for peace; without talking about Dubai's bankruptcy. Everybody is beautiful and life is fantastic!

In the meantime, a lot of scandals are exploding in France: Clearstream, CPE, divisions inside the left and right wings etc...The CPE (partial employment contract), instead of placating the underprivileged youth, stirs protests and strikes. Evidently, with a CPE you have to prove yourself and work hard to convince the company that you are a good asset. It's so hard to be a man! Values concerning family, work and morale are now only old clichés and I must be very old fashioned. The French want everything for nothing, but wait; we forget, they have democracy therefore they have the right to revolt! France is still a very nice country, but it has begun to fade into the historical heritage. People will come to visit the nice monuments, to enjoy the incredible culture, to kiss on the Pont Neuf, to eat some Camembert, to taste the snails and the frog legs (if it still exists) and to take a picture of the native survivors of a prehistoric era.

About USA, they think they have the hegemony over the world (try to understand the American logic, it's funnier than Sudoku, level very hard) but some time ago they were undergoing a series of mistakes, lies and scandals. For example, the murders of Iraqi civilians at Haditha: 24 innocents, women and children were assassinated at point blank by Marines who wanted to take revenge for one of their own killed in an explosion. Bravo, that was real courage!

The economic recession has plunged the USA into depths rarely reached, not to mention the subprime nonsense, the Madoff affair (he was recruiting most of his clients in the synagogue, I guess it is Jewish solidarity), mismanagement of the relief supplies for the victims of Katarina in Louisiana. The Bush administration cut off all the social allowances previously established, but increased the price of gasoline, electricity, food, education, insurance etc…Thank you so much; you really acted wisely and brightly. The Red Necks were enthusiastic in their mobile home, and then, they were the parents of soldiers gone to fight a war they no longer understood. A lot did not come back alive, but it's only war's casualties. Happily, Barak Obama has been elected and hope returned. I would not like to have his job because he has inherited a wounded country, hated by the rest of the world and still racist. Frankly, be obliged to produce his birth certificate! The poor man needs a lot of energy and will to restore the reputation of the USA and clean all the mess made by the previous Dalton's.

Lastly Asia and more specifically China, is truly happy. They invade the Western markets more and more and wait patiently for the explosion between the West and East. Their rule: wait for the right moment. It could be interesting when they'll move. We should, perhaps, learn Chinese to ease the communication.

CHAPTER 18

When Dubai holds us

IN DUBAI, I WAS lucky to meet people from every part of the world. The fact that people from 125 different countries lived together without conflict was an invaluable resource and a boundless hope for a better world. Very quickly I had to look closely at my own prejudices, and improve my tolerance threshold. I experienced different communication codes, either physical, oral or behavioral; beyond just learning a foreign language, I learned what adaptability means. At first, I was often shocked by those other ways of life, but with the time, although we had differences, I knew how to compromise and accept that we were all human beings with the same right to live.

A lot of us would like a better world, with peace, the eradication of poverty as well as of diseases and unfairness, and education for everyone; unfortunately we live in another reality far from our dreams.

Although I noted real social progress, there are still disparities between rich people and poor expatriates. As I wrote above, laborers are the new slaves, with ridiculous wages and extremely hard working conditions (a Westerner would not cope with it). Believe me, to build roads and buildings in the summertime are pretty awful. This shameful situation endures because, simply, those people have neither a choice, nor social or professional protection and, in their own country their families die of starvation or disease. Do you know this phrase: leave or die? In this story, the most disturbing thing is that those workers don't want to go back home; they take pride in being the provider for their relatives and they live for this honor. They know that in UAE there are no beggars; each one has a roof and something to eat. Although it is tough, their live depends on it.

When I went to India, what surprised me the most was the paradox between the misery of the population and their ability to smile and laugh, as being alive with their family was sufficient for their contentment. What a lesson of humility and wisdom I learned, as well as the answers to my questions, in the face of their tolerance and resignation. Equality will never exist; it's a lollipop promised to the masses in order to keep them quiet.

Nowadays, Dubai attracts a lot of businessmen and workers, because it is obliged to create some new concept to address its economical situation. In a dazzling way, I have seen the sand change into asphalt and the little roads, lined with palm trees and bougainvilleas, become five lane highways. The desert where camels were wandering became the sites for construction of buildings, able to compete with Singapore, Hong Kong or Kuala Lumpur. Late Sheikh Zayed Al Nayan planted a forest (several million Eucalyptus and Acacia trees) in the middle of the desert. When can we expect Napa Valley number two?

The Emiratis remain big kids and, their craziness is equal to their imagination: to build a marina in the desert, let's bring the water from the sea through canals! Enlarge the territory? Let's build artificial islands! Where is the problem? Most of the time, my daughter and I, are surprised and stunned by the speed of the growth, but at the same time, we regret the Dubai we knew during the nineties. It's like we have jumped a century ahead. From a quiet place with almost no development, we look at this exuberant evolution which challenges our adaptability. Evidently we are taking advantage of these new opportunities, but where are the dunes, the water falls in the mountains and the kindness of the Bedouins which seduced us?

I had found an oasis of peace and tranquility and now, I find myself in traffic jams that remind me the nightmare of driving in Paris. The mentalities change, the faces smile less, everything become more superficial and I fear that the gloomy atmosphere I fled is coming to pollute this country I love so much.

We were a small expatriate community, we knew each other and we came from around the world without any conflict. Today, Dubai is the "must go" destination, snobbism and arrogance abound. Relationships are now based upon a social and financial hierarchy. The "nouveaux riches" are everywhere and speak very loudly (they would like to be the elite, but you can't buy elegance and class). Even the parking valets fool themselves, if you want some attention, it's better to own a luxury car, otherwise you are ignored. My daughter has a lot of fun with her rental car (Honda Civic). She enjoys teasing the parking valet: when she gives the keys, she asks for special care for her expensive car. Normally, they get her sense of humor.

We don't talk anymore about dinners with friends but factual events where the women look like Christmas trees and the men like Casanova; funny, but so pathetic. Since the rumor that the Beckham family bought a villa in Dubai, the British suddenly reacquired their London Jet Set accent and, let's not forget that the late hybrid Michael Jackson settled for a while in Bahrain (about one hour flight from Dubai). Soon, we'll see Paris Hilton coming. In this case, I give up!

I was really fine here, I had split from the Parisian Jet Set and its emptiness; I came back to nature, to the principles forgotten by the vast West, and I was caught again in this exasperation. I love the fact that Dubai is stepping forward but I'd wish everything goes a little slower, a bit softer, kinder, safer and more peaceful, with the love of friends and family.

From now on, everything is getting worse, because Dubai could not escape the world crisis. Wanting to develop so fast, Dubai as been obliged to empty its pockets, consequently, 200,000 people already left the country, leaving their possessions and cars behind. The airport parking lot is now a big auction place where you can find any type of vehicle. Most of the construction projects have been stopped, leaving the workers to survive without wages.

Epilogue

Camille has lived a tranquil and joyful childhood to the point she feels she belongs to the UAE. Her roots are unmistakably Middle Eastern and even, she went through some painful moments, but the sweet way of live did ease her way a lot. Each time she returns"to home" as she says, she rediscovers with joy her friends, her landmarks and her memories. She is now an American student, finishing her MBA, and she tries her best to teach others what really are the Middle East and the Arabs; she fights racism and exclusion. Perhaps, she'll go back to Dubai for a job. She will be disappointed for sure by the working environment, but she will have the opportunity to continue her experience. Now diplomas are not enough to tackle life; henceforth you should be strong, feet well rooted in the ground and have nerves of steel to face today's reality. The Middle East can teach you that, plus the patience.

My time n Dubai was unforgettable with the exposure to multiple identities. They are a proud people which cling to its freedom. The Middle East is known for its unwillingness to follow orders and rules where religion is not at play, and yet…The main contradiction is between their will for peace and their inner rebellion. They are perpetually stretched between the quest of pleasure and serenity and their inability to obey. It is not easy to establish a structure where things are organized in a logical way. That may be why setting up democracy is such a challenge. The Arabs are in the first instances traditionalists, who don't cope easily with the hazards and obligations that modernity and new technology bring. To cope with the inconvenience of globalization and development is not their cup of tea.

With its architecture, Dubai looks like a futuristic city, but its mentality still remains old-fashioned. The rulers have a long-term vision of exponential growth, but I am afraid this will entail managing some very complicated situations. The territory is small, which explains the strict rules for owning property: the building, yes, the land, no.

The escalation of prices has started to eliminate a certain part of the expatriate community; of course the basic jobs are greatly impacted. Simply put, in the future I don't see the development of infrastructure growth without the workers who enable it to be implemented.

At last, international trade and the establishment of foreign companies here mean that foreigners will acquire a true decision-making power in this country, and thereby a political voice. Is not it difficult to manage a country which is no longer yours? For the moment, it's like a huge auction of the UAE. I have the feeling there will be some harsh steps to climb. Already, a new fact: certain wealthy and influent expatriates are acquiring citizenship (especially rich Indians and Middle Easterners). They must absolutely find a solution for maintaining the Emirati national identity.

I was enchanted by the East, by its softness, its values. The beauty and purity of landscapes was sublime. I saw and I learned so many things through the people I met. I appreciated the pride with which this people faced the ups and downs of life. They knew how to temper my rebelliousness, to make me lovable and patient, and to teach me the spirituality of the Whole and of the moment.

The world is beautiful, touching and interesting by virtue of its diversity. There is injustice, crime, corruption and unbelievable cruelty, but also a wealth, a source of unlimited knowledge and infinite human resources.

We have to control our urge to dominate and to stop believing we are eternal and living Gods, holding the universal truth. I naively assume that our life today has always been thus; who will stop human beings, crazy about power, wealth and influence? Who will erase the envy, the jealousy, the lack of self esteem and the psychological misery? We have to accept the inevitable. The elite who govern the world are humans of flesh-and-blood, few of whom have a long-term global vision of mankind. They mostly seek satisfaction of their desires for possessions and glory, where their ego is controlling their actions; they place no value on moral and ethical principles and their negative consequences. It must be a jubilating experience to own a country and its people must it not?

I'd like to remember the awesome moments I've had in France when politics were still sensible, rather than egotistic and inept. When the political winter descended, like a cicada, I left to sing elsewhere.

In the UAE, sometimes I sang sad songs, but most of the time they were joyful. For the rest of my life I'll remain grateful for that.